Praise for

Defensive Design
for the Web

"The best-laid plans of mice and web developers often go awry. No matter how artfully you structure, write, and design your company's site, someone is always going to hit the wrong button, type the wrong password, or make other normal human mistakes. Anticipating errors and helping customers bounce back into the site's flow can make the difference between success and failure. This clear, easy-to-read book tells how, with a depth no related title can match. Buy it; read it; keep it close to your monitor. The customer relationship you save may be your own."

Jeffrey Zeldman
Author, *Designing with Web Standards*

"*Defensive Design for the Web* shows you how to create a good customer experience even when things go wrong. If you work in user experience or usability, you have to learn what's in this book."

Mark Hurst
Founder, Creative Good
Author, *Good Experience* newsletter

"Defend yourself—listen to 37signals! If useful web design is important to you, then how can you NOT pay attention to Defensive Design? Matt and Jason break new ground on a crucial part of web design that you don't hear much about elsewhere."

Scott Heiferman
Co-Founder, Meetup.com & Fotolog.net

Defensive Design
for the Web

How to Improve Error Messages,
Help, Forms, and Other Crisis Points

37signals

Matthew Linderman
with Jason Fried

New
Riders

1249 Eighth Street, Berkeley, California 94710
An imprint of Peachpit,
A division of Pearson Education

DEFENSIVE DESIGN FOR THE WEB
How to improve error messages, help, forms,
and other crisis points

International Standard Book Number: 0-7357-1410-X

Library of Congress Catalog Card Number: 2003111678

Printed in the United States of America

First printing: March, 2004

06   7 6 5

Trademarks

Warning and Disclaimer

Associate Publisher
Stephanie Wall

Production Manager
Gina Kanouse

Senior Development Editor
Jennifer Eberhardt

Senior Project Editor
Lori Lyons

Copy Editor
Keith Cline

Indexer
Julie Bess

Composition
Kim Scott

Manufacturing Coordinator
Dan Uhrig

Interior Designer
Kim Scott

Cover Designers
Matthew Linderman
Ryan Singer

Cover Production
Aren Howell

Marketing
Scott Cowlin
Tammy Detrich

Publicity Manager
Susan Nixon

TABLE OF CONTENTS

CHAPTER THREE

Language Matters
PROVIDE CLEAR INSTRUCTIONS **36**

CHAPTER FOUR

Bulletproof Forms
CREATE FRIENDLY FORMS THAT ARE EASY TO COMPLETE   **56**

CHAPTER FIVE

Missing in Action
OVERCOME MISSING PAGES, IMAGES, OR PLUG-INS   **90**

ABOUT 37SIGNALS

Matthew Linderman

Jason Fried

Chicago-based **37signals** (www.37signals.com) is a team of web design and usability specialists dedicated to simple, and usable, customer-focused design. 37signals popularized the concept of contingency/defensive design in various articles and white papers and via the web site DesignNotFound.com. The team also has conducted workshops and presentations on the topic for a variety of conferences and companies.

37signals clients include Microsoft, Qwest, Monster.com, Clear Channel, Panera Bread, Meetup, Performance Bike, and Transportation.com. Work has been featured in the *New York Times*, *Sports Illustrated*, *Washington Post*, on *CNN*, and in numerous other publications. Team members have appeared as featured speakers at AIGA Risk/Reward, Activ8, South By Southwest, HOW Design Conference, ForUse, and other conferences. Additional information can be found at www.37signals.com.

This book is authored by **Matthew Linderman** with **Jason Fried**. Other members of the 37signals team include Ryan Singer and Scott Upton.

ABOUT THE TECHNICAL REVIEWER

 **Toby Braun** is a freelance information designer who specializes in information architecture and interface design for the web (www.tbid.com). His design style is typified by the terms *simplicity*, *ease of use*, and *legibility*. In a previous life as a senior-level advertising art director, Toby was an early evangelist of computer-aided design and interactive marketing strategies. He has given lectures at MIT's Media Lab, Columbia College, and The School of the Art Institute of Chicago. Toby's work and essays have been featured on web sites such as IEEE Spectrum Online, ProjectCool.com, and Suck.com; as well as in *Information Week*, *Yahoo! Internet Life*, and *Entertainment Weekly* magazines. He has more than 20 years of design experience.

Toby lives in Chicago with his wife, Ilana, and his two children, Theo and Lola. Toby likes to collect cookbooks and cameras. He tries to practice yoga daily (and if he doesn't, he gets kinda grumpy).

ACKNOWLEDGMENTS

Thanks to everyone whose inspiration and support helped make this book a possibility, including the Frieds, the Lindermans, Scott Upton, Ernest Kim, Ryan Singer, Michael Nolan, Jennifer Eberhardt, Stephanie Wall, everyone at New Riders, Toby Braun, 37signals clients, David Heinemeier Hansson, Jeffrey Zeldman, Jason Kottke, Hugh Forrest, Richard Bird, Carlos Segura, Brin Lorenc, Edmund Burke, Jakob Nielsen, Steven Garrity, Maggie Berry, Charles Foreman, Jim Coudal, everyone at Coudal Partners, Pamela LiCalzi O'Connell, Joyce Berlinsky, Ann Rosenblum, Sue Garibaldi, Matt Ruby, Dave Skwarczek, Stewart Butterfield, Doc Searls, Scott Heiferman, Krista Moscarello, Jason Roberts, Don Schenck, Zoran Svetlicic, Leslie Townley, Jamie Tibbetts, Josh Ulm, Ammon Haggerty, Noah Dan, George Vuckovic, Don Schnitzius, James Cicenia, Ted Billups, Crystal Yednak, Dan Arkind, Mark Hurst, Luke Wroblewski, Joshua Kaufman, Ilise Benun, Curt Cloninger, Daniel Graham, Dara Sahebjami, Jeffrey Veen, Steve Krug, Nametron 3000, eNormicom, our weblog friends, the Signals vs. Noise community, and the Design Not Found community.

TELL US WHAT YOU THINK

As the reader of this book, you are the most important critic and commentator. We value your opinion and want to know what we're doing right, what we could do better, what areas you'd like to see us publish in, and any other words of wisdom you're willing to pass our way.

When you contact us, please be sure to include this book's title, ISBN, and author, as well as your name and email address. We will carefully review your comments and share them with the author and editors who worked on the book.

Email: errata@newriders.com

Chapter One

UNDERSTANDING DEFENSIVE DESIGN

Making mistakes well

Imagine this:

Scenario 1

You're at a department store and you ask for a mop. But the clerk sends you to the electronics section.

Scenario 2

You call your travel agent to get help with a lost ticket. But you're forced to listen to ads for 5 minutes before you get any assistance.

Scenario 3

You go to an electronics store to fix a problem with your TV. But the store's representative is able to answer you only with arcane industry acronyms such as MTS, PIP, INVAR, and SRS.

Sound farfetched? Unfortunately, these sorts of customer service failures are all too common online. Let's take a look.

www.target.com

A search for "mop" at Target returns a list of electronic appliances but no mops.

www.orbitz.com

Make a mistake at Orbitz and a large ad banner overshadows the text that indicates something went wrong.

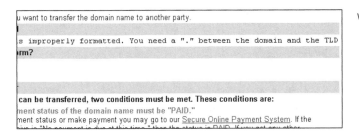

www.networksolutions.com

Problems registering a domain at Network Solutions? They'll confuse you further with esoteric acronyms such as TLD.

NO ONE'S PERFECT

Let's admit it: Things will go wrong online. No matter how carefully you design a site, no matter how much testing you do, customers will still encounter problems. Sites must plan for these inevitable breakdowns with defensive design. This book will show you how.

By improving defensive design, online businesses can help customers recover from mishaps—increasing conversion rates and customer loyalty in the process.

WHY "DEFENSIVE DESIGN"?

The title is inspired by the concept of defensive driving (that is, recognizing potential accident situations developing and taking advance measures to avoid them). The same way a driver must always be on the lookout for slick roads, reckless drivers, and other dangerous scenarios, site builders must constantly search for trouble spots that may cause visitors confusion and frustration. Good site defense can make or break the customer experience.

Contingency Design

Defensive design is also often referred to as contingency design (as in planning for all contingencies). Throughout the rest of this book, we use the term contingency design to describe the concept.

CRISIS POINTS

Crisis points—the screens people see when things go wrong.

Anyone who has spent time online has experienced these sorts of problems:

> "This isn't what I searched for."

> "Did my order go through?"

> "How do I get out of here?"

> "Where is the page I clicked on?"

Here are some typical crisis points:

- Form error
- Page Not Found error
- Server error

- Help Screen
- Inaccurate search results
- Out-of-stock item

Why are they important? These screens are where frustrated customers are most likely to abandon a site. If they can't figure out what to do next or they don't understand what's happening, they'll often give up. In other words, a crisis point may be your last chance to retain a customer on the edge.

It happens

Online crisis points are impossible to avoid entirely. Sources include the following:

- A server malfunction
- A code bug
- Browser incompatibility
- Failed Internet connection
- Unclear language
- Confusing design
- Sloppy forms
- Pages that have been moved, deleted, or renamed
- Countless other possibilities…

The Sad Truth

"Let's acknowledge a sad truth about software: Any code of significant scope and power will have bugs in it. Even a relatively simple software product today has millions of lines of code that provide many places for bugs to hide. That's why our customers still encounter bugs despite the rigorous and extensive stress testing and beta testing we do."

—Steve Ballmer, CEO Microsoft[1]

"Anything that can possibly go wrong, will go wrong."

—Murphy's law

---

[1] "Microsoft Reports Progress in Averting Computer Crashes," *New York Times* (October, 2002)

Overcoming crisis points

There are three common results when a customer encounters a crisis point:

1. The customer gives up and bails out.
2. The customer deals, but becomes frustrated and jaded.
3. The customer is helped back on track and has a satisfying customer experience.

Getting the right result (3) isn't always as easy as it seems, however.

Why? One big reason is that site builders don't realize what it's like for outsiders to use their site. Many make the mistake of thinking, "If I can overcome this obstacle, so can everyone else."

That's simply not the case. Because you're reading this book, chances are you're a somewhat experienced web surfer and can overcome most online difficulties. It would be a mistake to think all visitors are just as savvy or patient, however. Technically inclined people represent only a tiny percentage of those who use the web. For regular folks, the aforementioned crisis points can be quite confusing and intimidating.

This confusion often leads to dire consequences:

- Abandoned shopping carts
- Failed registrations
- Irrelevant search results
- Increased support inquiries
- Customer frustration
- Customer bailouts

CONTINGENCY DESIGN TO THE RESCUE

That's why it's critical to use contingency design to help customers overcome crisis points.

Contingency design—design for when things go wrong.

This book will teach you all about contingency design, design for when things go wrong. To be more specific, contingency design is the error messaging, graphic design, programming, instructive text, information architecture, and customer service that prevents errors and helps visitors get back on track after a problem occurs.

Effective contingency design...

- Helps prevent errors before they occur.
- Helps get people back on track smoothly if an error does occur.
- Shows you care by helping people when they need help most.

Examples of successful contingency design

- An error message that clearly explains how to fix the problem
- A form field that prevents a visitor from entering too many characters
- A form that validates responses before they are accepted
- Customized "Page Not Found" screen that explains the problem and helps people get to the desired page
- Contextual help (definitions and inline FAQs that answer questions on the spot)
- Login help (for instance, "Forget your password? Click here.")
- Help copy that doesn't require a dictionary or technical manual to understand
- FAQs that solve the most common problems that plague customers
- A smart search engine that understands misspellings and other common errors
- Email notification for the return of an out-of-stock item

Real-World Contingency Design

Many offline industries already understand the importance of contingency design. You're probably already familiar with these real-world examples of contingency design:

• Spare tire	• Fire extinguisher
• Smoke alarm	• Airbag
• Road signs (for example, "Slippery When Wet")	• Seat belt
• TV closed captioning	• Plane seat cushion as flotation device
• Life jacket	• Childproof containers
• Bulletproof vest	• Gas mask
• Parachute	• Life boat
• First aid kit	

SUCCESS STORIES

Does contingency design really make a difference? Let's take a look at how some smart companies have used the techniques found in this book to improve their sites.

www.landsend.com

Lands' End decided it could do more than just display the typical "out-of-stock" message for an unavailable item. The site also presents alternative items that are available immediately. The site also lets people backorder unavailable items. The conversion rate at LandsEnd.com is 11 percent, one of the highest among online apparel retailers.[2] Site creators say that this sort of dedication to the customer is a major reason why.[3]

---

[2] "Top 20 Web Retailers," PC Data (October 2000)

[3] "E-Tailers Beef Up Online Support To Corral Carts and Shoppers," *InternetRetailer* (June 2001)

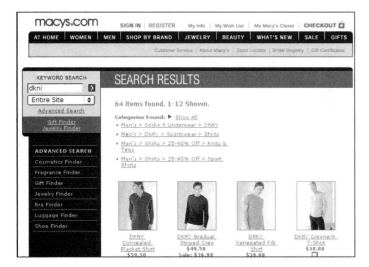

www.macys.com

Macy's more than doubled the rate at which it converts site visitors into buyers by effectively planning for inaccurate search queries. For example, mistakenly enter "DKNI" and the site still returns results for DKNY (the correct spelling). Macy's executives said that planning for this contingency has led to a big boost in the site's conversion rate.[4]

www.google.com

Google found that a large percentage of customers were complaining about inaccurate results when a search term was misspelled. This surprised site staffers because Google offers a spell-check feature. A study of site traffic revealed customers were missing the

---

[4] "Macy's Doubles Conversion Rate," *InternetWeek* (November 2001)

"Did you mean to search for ____?" link at the top of the page. Therefore, Google decided to repeat the correction on the bottom of the page (next to the link for complaints). Since then usage of the correction link has doubled.[5]

These are just a few examples that demonstrate how planning for failure can result in clear improvements in usability and conversion rates.

Smooth Recoveries

Customers know better than to always expect a 100-percent problem-free experience. That's why they value companies that plan for failure and provide successful recoveries. Here's another offline example to illustrate the point:

A customer study at a global hotel chain demonstrated the importance of providing effortless recoveries. Guests who experienced a problem that was quickly and politely resolved rated the hotel service *higher* than guests who had no problems at all. And guests with happy resolution of their hassle were *more likely* to recommend the hotel than trouble-free guests.[6] Although it may seem counterintuitive to many businesses, customers are likely to remember a graceful rescue and overlook the problem that necessitated it.

Other Real-World Smooth Recoveries

- An airline provides a free travel voucher to a passenger bumped from a crowded flight.
- A restaurant provides a free dessert to compensate for a bad meal.
- A retailer allows a return despite a missing receipt.

SO WHAT WILL THIS BOOK TEACH ME?

This book will show you how to use contingency design to improve your site's usability. You'll learn the following:

- What contingency design is and why it's important
- 40 guidelines that will help you prevent errors and rescue customers when things go wrong
- How to make error recovery and prevention part of your long-term design process
- How to evaluate your site's contingency design so you can focus on the areas that need help most

---

[5] "Monitoring the online customer experience," *Good Experience* (October, 2002)
[6] "Make No Mistake?" *Fortune* (December 2001)

WHAT WON'T I LEARN FROM THIS BOOK?

It's impossible to be all things to all readers, so let's also be clear about what this book won't do. For one thing, it won't provide specific recommendations on software or platforms to use for your site. There aren't many one-size-fits-all solutions in web design and development, so this book purposely avoids endorsing specific products.

Also, this book does not contain in-depth programming examples or code snippets. Although there are occasional notes on how to approach implementation, you'll find general guidance rather than specific solutions (which vary widely depending on your site's specific needs and resources).

WHO SHOULD READ IT?

Anyone who wants to improve the customer experiences at a web site, including:

- **Designers and information architects**
  See screenshots, case studies, and layout techniques that help visitors overcome problems.
- **Developers**
  See how leading sites deal with form validation, 404s, and other common errors.
- **Copywriters**
  See how clear copy keeps customers informed and on track.
- **Project managers and executives**
  Learn how a top-down commitment and interdepartmental cooperation can deliver bottom-line results.

HOW SHOULD I USE THIS BOOK?

The bulk of this book is made up of contingency design guidelines that can improve your site. Read through these guidelines and study the examples. Along the way, you'll come up with plenty of ideas for improving your site. If you're short on time, go ahead and make these changes while you're reading through the text. Otherwise, take your time and focus on grasping the concepts underlying effective contingency design.

After you've completed reading the guidelines, perform the contingency design test located at the end of the book. This series of tasks will help you evaluate your site's contingency design and identify problem spots. You may also want to perform the test on outsiders (for instance, customers or other folks less familiar with your site than you).

After you've read the guidelines and completed the test, start modifying your site. The great thing about contingency design is that even small fixes can yield noticeable results. After you make the improvements, go back to the test and see how your site stands up. Keep at it until your site is in line with all the guidelines.

You also should continue to monitor your site after corrections are made. As your site evolves, new problems may crop up.

You also can visit our site at www.DesignNotFound.com for additional contingency design examples and discussion.

A BRIEF INTRODUCTION TO THE GUIDELINES

The following chapters contain 40 contingency design principles for improving your site's usability. Before diving in, it's important for you to understand how the Guidelines sections work.

Each guideline includes the following:

- **Summary**
  An explanation of what the guideline means and why it's important.

- **Positive ("Thumbs Up") example(s)**
  A visual example (with description) of a site that follows the guideline. Thumbs Up examples show the benefits of following the guideline. When appropriate, the description also offers ways that the site in question can further improve its contingency design.

- **Negative ("Thumbs Down") example(s)**
  A visual example (with description) of a site that doesn't follow the guideline. Thumbs Down examples show the dangers of ignoring the relevant guideline. Often, we'll suggest ideas for improvement. Also, note that many of these sites will have already improved by the time you read this book. However, similar issues are usually replicated throughout the web, so the point is still relevant.

Many guidelines also contain the following:

- **As If analogies**
  A real-world analogy to help you understand the example in the context of an offline situation. For example, an As If might compare shopping at Gap.com to shopping at your local mall's Gap.

- **Customer quotes**

  Perspectives from real people on what it's like to experience the sort of good/bad contingency design featured in the example. These quotes come from DesignNotFound.com, a site that enables visitors to comment on contingency design examples from around the web.

- **Head to Head examples**

  A side-by-side comparison of how two different sites, often from the same industry, handle the same issue. One site follows the guideline, one site doesn't.

BE FLEXIBLE

Keep in mind that when it comes to web usability, there are no hard-and-fast rules. In some instances, your site may be better off not following a guideline. Just make sure you have a good reason for doing so.

ONE LAST THING: SEE PEOPLE, NOT USERS

Before we move on, there's one more thing. Actually it's something you *won't* see in this book: the word *users*.

Users sounds like a bunch of junkies or gigolos. The people who visit web sites aren't users, click throughs, hits, numbers on a spreadsheet, or some other form of dehumanizing jargon. They're your husband, your mom, your friend, the guy who sits in the cubicle next to you. They're real *people*, just like you and I.

That's why we say *visitors*, *customers*, or just plain 'ol *people*. Sure it's a small thing, but the message is significant; contingency design requires a focus on the human beings in trouble at the other end of your site. They're lost, confused, or frustrated and they need your help. It's all about treating these people with the respect they deserve.

LET'S GET TO IT

All right, we've set the table. Now let's get to the main course: the guidelines.

Chapter Two

SHOW THE PROBLEM
Display obvious error messages and alerts

Guidelines covered in this chapter

1. Give an error message that's noticeable at a glance.

2. Use color, icons, and text to clearly highlight and explain the problem area.

3. Always identify errors the same way.

4. Eliminate the need for back-and-forth clicking.

INTRODUCTION

Regardless of how usable your site is, mistakes will occur. When things do go wrong, help your visitors quickly grasp the situation and potential solutions with a clear, helpful error message.

A good error message lets a customer instantly know

1. That an error occurred
2. What the error is
3. How to recover

When handled properly, error messages are only a slight hiccup in the customer experience; customers spot the foul and quickly rectify the problem. If a site fails to clearly display or explain an error, however, there's a good chance that customers will abandon the site, potentially for good.

You can use the guidelines in this chapter to make identifying and correcting errors a no-brainer.

GUIDELINE 1

Give an error message that's noticeable at a glance

It may seem obvious, but you actually have to tell people when an error occurs. Many people speed through sites and often can't even tell a breakdown has occurred. It's your job to make sure they immediately recognize, even at a glance, that an error has occurred. Provide a clear indication that an error has occurred along with text that describes the problem and how to solve it. An alert icon can also help draw attention to the problem area.

QwestDex

WHERE'S MY ERROR MESSAGE?   www.qwestdex.com

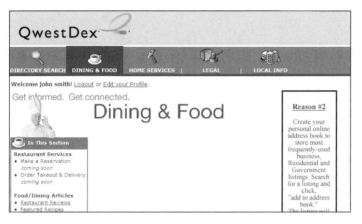

I went to the "Dining & Food" section of QwestDex's yellow pages site and searched for restaurant reviews. The problem? I forgot to enter a state. Instead of indicating any error, the site returned a page with *no content* in the body section.

An empty page just doesn't cut it. QwestDex should provide an error message that tells me the search can't be completed and why (in this case, the state was omitted). Then, Qwest should provide a clear path to rectify the problem (for instance, a pull-down menu that lets me select a state and then continue my search). QwestDex would also be wise to allow site visitors to provide feedback at this and other points of failure.

Hilton

BUT I JUST ENTERED MY LOGIN   www.hilton.com

I entered an incorrect username while signing in at Hilton's site. Instead of indicating an error, the site simply asks me to re-enter my information again. The site doesn't come right out and tell me there's a problem. Did something go wrong or do I just need to re-enter the information for verification? Because the message isn't clear, I try again only to wind up facing the same confusing situation again.

The site should indicate the error instead of just displaying the same sign-in form again. A more helpful message might read, "You entered an invalid username and/or password. Please check your spelling and try again or click here to get help."

I tried to go directly to Mother Nature's "Top Sellers" area by entering "http://www.mothernature.com/topsellers" into my browser. It turns out this is the wrong URL.

How does the site handle this mistake? Instead of providing a "Page not found" error message, the site automatically redirects me to the home page.

Although this may seem like a helpful move, it actually frustrates me because I'm looking for "Top Sellers," not the home page. Without an explanation, I have no idea what happened or why I was sent to a different page than the one I requested. The site should create a customized "Page not found" screen for customers who wind up at invalid URLs (see Guideline 16 in Chapter 5).

Don't force your customers to become detectives. Visitors won't stick around to piece together error clues—they'll just give up.

KB Toys

OBVIOUS ERROR NOTICE   www.kbtoys.com

KB Toys provides an obvious error notice at the top of the page that identifies a problem with my shipping address. This yellow box with bold red text is the sort of "can't-miss" notification style you should use at your site. An alert icon would help the message stand out even more.

Excite

TRY AGAIN ERROR   www.excite.com

Excite handles a failed login properly. The site explains that an invalid member name was entered and then politely asks visitors to try again. This stacks up nicely when compared to the Hilton example shown previously that merely told visitors to re-enter information without explaining why.

GUIDELINE 2

Use color, icons, and text to clearly highlight and explain the problem area

So what is the best way to inform customers of an error? Make sure your error messages follow these rules:

1. Clearly state the error at the top of the page *and* at the problem area that needs to be corrected.
2. Indicate the problem area with bold red text.
3. Draw attention to the problem area with an alert icon or other graphical cue.
4. Offer possible solutions to the problem.
5. Don't force visitors to retype data entered correctly.

Topica
THE WRONG WAY   www.topica.com

Topica gives me an alert icon, but where's the text to explain the problem? Without an explanation, this error notification isn't very helpful.

Sony
WRONG SPOT   www.sony.com

Sony's error message is confusing because it is nowhere near the problem area that needs to be corrected. (That is, username, the field that needs to be fixed, is at the top of the screen **[A]**, whereas the error is near the bottom of the screen **[B]**.) This poor messaging is bound to create further confusion.

The site shouldn't make people hunt for the problem. Instead, the error notification should appear adjacent to the area that needs to be fixed.

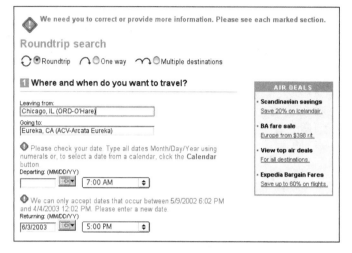

Expedia shows us the right way to display error messages. The site...

1. Displays an error message at the top of the screen and at the specific problem fields.

2. Uses bold red text to explain the problem.

3. Provides a clear error icon that is easily noticed at the top of the page and at the specific problem fields.

4. Explains each individual problem and how to fix it.

5. Saves the location data so it doesn't need to be retyped.

Google
CAN'T-MISS ERROR MESSAGE   www.google.com

In this image, Google shows us one way to successfully associate an error message with the field in question. Red boxes enclose the fields that need to be fixed along with their respective error messages. Google realizes that both the content *and* location of an error message matter.

Banana Republic
CLEAR EXPLANATION   www.bananarepublic.com

I entered a zip code that was one digit short at Banana Republic's site. The site highlights the field and concisely explains the acceptable zip code formats. Is anything missing? An icon would help draw attention to the message.

GUIDELINE 3

Always identify errors the same way

When customers see how an error is handled, they'll expect a similar response to future errors. That's why you should always identify errors in a predictable, consistent manner. Use the same colors, alerts, fonts, text, and tone when explaining errors. You should also place error messages in the same spot on each page.

Customers appreciate consistency because it saves them time and energy. It also instills a sense of trust because it demonstrates that a unified company operates the site. Faced with inconsistent messages, customers are liable to think one area of a company doesn't know what the other is doing.

E*Trade's "Banking" and "Financial" sections present me with inconsistent styles for error messages. This is bad because it forces me to notice different styles of error messages—increasing the likelihood that I'll miss one. E*Trade should pick one notification method and go with it.

It's also worth noting that error messages are an important part of brand communication. An inconsistent tone of voice or graphic style at crisis points can have a negative impact on your brand's identity.

As if...

Why is this bad? It's as if the stop signs in one state are red octagons but in the next state they're blue rectangles.

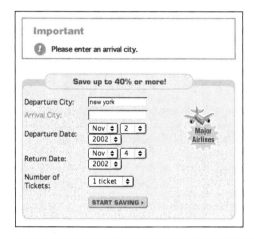

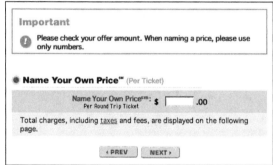

Priceline makes sure that errors are always displayed the same way. A yellow box with an orange alert and black explanatory text is displayed if you make a mistake entering an arrival city or naming a price. This consistency improves the odds that a customer will spot the error and recover gracefully.

GUIDELINE 4

Eliminate the need for back-and-forth clicking

Many sites make the mistake of forcing customers to go back and forth between pages to correct errors. Whenever possible, collect errors and display them on a page that allows visitors to fix mistakes without backtracking.

Another approach is to narrow the scope of the page so that customers aren't faced with the entire form again. If only one field is problematic and requires attention, why risk confusing or intimidating visitors by showing them the entire form again? Accept the valid information entered and show a page where only the problem field is displayed.

Review and confirm your contact information		
Email address	jojo@imdb.com	To be verified via email
Full name	Jojo Schmidt	OK
Address		Invalid
City	New York	OK
State	NY	OK
Zip Code	10001	OK
Country	United States	OK
Primary phone #		Invalid
Date of Birth	Not Specified	OK

There are problems with the information you submitted.
Please click the Edit button below to make the corrections indicated.

Click [Edit] if you need to make any changes

I left some required fields blank during eBay's registration process. Instead of letting me fix the mistakes right away, eBay forces me to go back to the previous page to correct the invalid entries. This is especially annoying because the form page I return to doesn't contain the error information. This means I have to put forth extra effort to remember which fields are problematic.

eBay shouldn't put the onus on the customer to travel backward and recall problem fields. When a form error occurs, sites should redisplay the form with the problem fields clearly highlighted.

Shutterfly
NO MORE BACKTRACKING   www.shutterfly.com

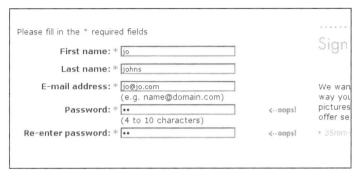

Shutterfly's one-page solution means I don't have to go back and forth to fix the error. I appreciate this technique because it minimizes the clicks required and doesn't force me to remember which entries are bogus.

Unfortunately, the cutesy "oops" labels do not provide any contextual help in tracking down what the problem is with the password fields. The site should go the extra mile and inform visitors of the specific problem. A better message would read, "You must select a password that is between 4 and 10 characters long."

United Airlines
WHICH AIRPORT IN CHICAGO?   www.ual.com

My destination entry at United's site wasn't specific enough. (I entered "Chicago,"—not enough information because the city has two airports.) Instead of displaying the entire form again, United saves my other information and presents only the problem field with an explanation. United even narrows down my choices to the two Chicago airports to eliminate the possibility of another invalid entry.

HEAD TO HEAD
Forgotten Form Field

I make a purchase at a web site for the first time. During registration, I miss a couple of required form fields.

 Ticketmaster   www.ticketmaster.com

---

ticketmaster

- You did not enter your first name. Please click "back" and enter it.
- You did not enter a valid credit card number. Please click "back" and correct it.

Back

©2001 Ticketmaster. All rights reserved.

I'm notified of the errors on a new page. To fix my mistakes, I have to go back to the registration page (which contains no indication of which fields need to be corrected).

By displaying the error message on a separate page, Ticketmaster forces me to go back a page to resolve the problem. Because that page does not display the error, I have to remember the contents of the error message after I leave this page. This method increases the workload on me and makes a bad situation even worse.

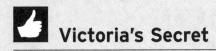

Victoria's Secret

www.victoriassecret.com

Checkout: Billing Address
U.S./Canada Billing Address

We're sorry. We need the following information... **A**

* First Name
* Confirm E-Mail

Non U.S./Canada billing address? click here

Military APO/FPO billing address? click here

Please enter your billing address.

* Required Fields **B**

First Name *   MI   Last Name *
                      Doe

Street Address * (Example: 1234 East Main Street Apt.1)
Main Street

Care Of or Business Name

I'm notified of my omissions both at the top of the page ("We're sorry …" **[A]**) and at the fields I left empty (the text above the problem fields are colored red rather than black **[B]**).

Victoria's Secret understands that purchasing online can be an intimidating experience and does all it can to help me through the process. I don't have to backtrack and I don't have to remember which fields were problematic because they're clearly noted. The only thing missing is an error icon to call attention to the bad field.

CHAPTER SUMMARY

Helpful error messaging is the first step toward getting troubled visitors back on track. State the error at the top of the page and also at the specific problem area. Use color, icons, and text to make spotting and fixing errors simple. Utilize consistent techniques while identifying errors. Also, make sure visitors don't have to backtrack to correct errors.

Chapter Three

LANGUAGE MATTERS
Provide clear instructions

Guidelines covered in this chapter

5 Don't use language that might be unfamiliar to your customers.

6 Keep text brief and easy to understand.

7 Be polite.

INTRODUCTION

Sure, you "get" your site's warnings and error messages. But how helpful are these messages for people outside your company? Can they understand the terms you use? Are they able to get back on track with your advice? Do they think the language is polite and well written?

Error messages and other contingency design text need to be helpful to everyone, not just site builders.

Amateurish error messages speak only to professionals. Professional error messages speak to amateurs.

Although clear, effective, polite language is important throughout your site, you should pay special attention to crisis point copy. Visitors who encounter crisis points are already frustrated and often on the verge of giving up. Unless they receive instructions that quickly explain and resolve the problem, they'll head for the nearest exit.

Unfortunately, many sites provide confusing directions, overly technical information, and unfamiliar terms when customers need help the most.

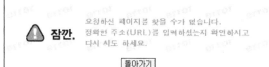

Are you speaking the same language as your customers? To a general audience, terms such as "internal error code," "file specification errors," or "default command" seem like a foreign tongue.

Why are unhelpful error messages so common? Many companies make the mistake of dumping these copywriting assignments on staffers who are inexperienced at communicating directly with customers. (For instance, an engineer used to writing code will wind up responsible for the additional task of writing explanatory text for site visitors.) Other companies neglect contingency design copy altogether and stick with whatever "out-of-the-box" text shows up. Frequently, the result is confusing messaging that is often more harmful than helpful.

As with other important areas of your site, crisis points require writers who can *concisely and effectively speak in terms your audience can understand*. Visitors in trouble desperately need clear, helpful instructions. That's why contingency design copy is just as important, if not more so, than home page text or marketing content; make sure you give it adequate attention.

The following sections discuss writing tips that are especially important for crisis points.

GUIDELINE 5

Don't use language that might be unfamiliar to your customers

Can your Mom understand your site's contingency design text? How about your grand-mother? Or your 12 year old? If not, ask yourself how you can simplify the copy so that *everyone* gets the point.

Crisis points are frequently bogged down with language familiar only to the site's own staffers. Other times these screens are filled with technical terms recognizable only to developers and webheads. Contingency design copy needs to speak to ordinary customers, not just these specialized groups.

Use terms that all visitors can comprehend. Stay away from obscure codes, abbreviations, technical jargon, or internal marketing terms unfamiliar to your customers. Use plain English that's easy to grasp, even for visitors who are not technically oriented.

OOPS!

Your Team: Marvin Gardens
Your League: The Football League of Canada

Could not continue scan with NOLOCK due to data movement. Severity 12, State 3, Procedure 'SPORTSQL02 sp_getOrderedTeamData', Line 58

Click the "Back" button on your browser to return to the previous page.

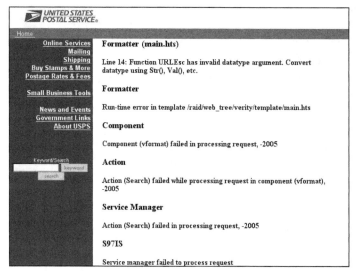

Server-side errors at the ESPN and U.S. Post Office sites result in these worthless messages. Why are ordinary visitors seeing this technical information? Text such as "NOLOCK due to data movement" and "invalid datatype argument" means nothing to the average Joe.

You've got to remember that regular folks don't speak the same language as your site's staffers or back-end systems. Don't show obtuse technical error information to customers. Databases and programming languages often generate standard errors such as the ones shown above to report on system failures. Make sure you catch these messages and tailor them to the appropriate audience. Detailed technical content may be helpful to the site development team, but it will simply confuse most visitors. *Error messages must illuminate, not confound.*

Current WHOIS record
This domain name is improperly formatted. You need a "." between the domain and the TLD

Sites should also refrain from using unexplained acronyms or industry jargon. In this case, Network Solutions casually uses the acronym "TLD" without ever defining it. This is a problem because Jane Q. Customer may have no idea what "TLD" means. (FYI: It actually stands for top-level domain.) Sites should explain any acronym that may be unfamiliar to a large percentage of visitors. Alternatively, resist the acronym urge altogether.

From the customer...

"This is another example of a company using its internal technical terms where it shouldn't—usually easily solved by using an actual writer for error messages, instead of allowing the developer to write the text."

Switchboard
KEEP INTERNAL TERMS INTERNAL

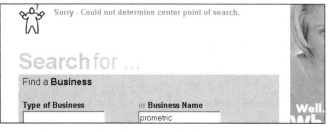

There's a problem with my "center point of search." But what's that? Switchboard staffers may know, but does anyone else? A more customer-centric message would read, "A city is required to complete this search. Please enter one below."

As if...

Why is this bad? It's as if I call up information to get a number. Instead of asking which city I want to search, the operator asks me for my "target radius."

From the customer...

"This is a battle we fight constantly with the business experts in our company—using your internal terminology with your external users. It's pervasive online.

"But I was surprised to have it happen the other day at a brick 'n mortar Crate and Barrel. I wanted to know how expensive it would be to have something shipped to me since I wasn't sure if it would fit in my car. The clerk pulls out a binder and asks me 'What's your shipping zone?' My first instinct was to reply 'Umm...hell...27?!?' (I would've been wrong—turns out it was 3.)"

Typebox
ADD TO BUYBOX?

www.typebox.com

Step 3: To edit your order, add another copy of the same font, or view the itemization of your purchases, click "checkout your buybox". Remember: "Buybox" is the metaphor Typebox uses instead of 'shopping cart'.

At Typebox, a shopping cart isn't a shopping cart. It's a "Buybox." Bad idea. This cute term may seem like a good way to stand out from the crowd, but in truth it merely causes confusion. Typebox would be wise to stick with the traditional "Shopping Cart" label along with a cart icon.

University of Chicago
FUNKY ACRONYMS EXPLAINED

web-resources.uchicago.edu

What do all those funky web acronyms stand for?

Document Types

HTML (hypertext markup language) is the most common markup language used to create web pages. HTML is a subset of SGML (Standard Generalized Markup Language) and is used to create hypertext and hypermedia documents on the World Wide Web incorporating text, graphics, sound, video, and hyperlinks.

dHTML (dynamic **HTML**) is a collective term for a combination of new HTML tags and options that will let you create web pages that are more animated and more responsive to user interaction than previous versions of HTML. Much of dynamic HTML is specified in HTML 4.0. Features include an object-oriented view of a Web page and its elements; cascading style sheets and the layering of content; programming that can address all or most page elements; and dynamic fonts. DHTML can also produce Web documents that look and act like desktop applications or multimedia productions.

A **rollover** is a widely used dHTML effect. The dHTML rollover (also called a **mouseover**) works by switching the visibility of a CSS layer from hidden to visible and back again. This kind of rollover allows you to swap in text or plug-ins, as well as alternate back and forth between images to create the effect.

XML (extensible markup language) is used primarily for web pages and applications. XML allows content to be abstracted away from formatting, thus producing a single tagged document, which may then be displayed in a number of different formats (depending on the XSLT stylesheet used). An author could then extend and customize basic HTML formatting by creating proprietary tags and text behaviors. XML is meant to emphasize intelligent and logical formatting within technical documents in order to streamline searching and categorizing, and to ensure total cross-browser compatibility.

Even web experts get confused by all the acronyms flying around at technical sites. That's why the University of Chicago's web resources site provides a page that explains the "funky web acronyms" used throughout the site. Not sure what "XML" or "rollover" means? Click the term and you'll wind up at this handy glossary page that offers definitions in plain English.

GUIDELINE 6

Keep text brief and easy to understand

At crisis points, customers want to *quickly* know what went wrong and how to fix it. Don't force them to read an essay when a short note will suffice.

Use these tips to make your crisis point text helpful:

1. Lead with a clear headline and the most important information.
2. Offer bullet points rather than blocks of text.
3. Use bold text and color variation to highlight crucial information.
4. Edit copy so that it's brief yet meaningful.

Aer Lingus and Fortune

IS THERE AN ECHO IN HERE?   www.aerlingus.com and www.fortune.com

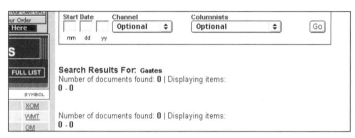

In these examples, Aer Lingus and Fortune each repeat error information unnecessarily. Most likely these sites use templates that neglect to factor in error contingencies such as those shown here. The result? Redundancy that adds confusion and makes visitors read extra text for no good reason. Smart sites say it once and then get out of the way.

The Motley Fool's "File not found" screen uses simple language that clearly explains the problem and answers the question "So now what?"

- The reason for the message is clearly stated at the beginning: "This page is not here." **[A]**

- The site uses a numbered list and bullet points for easy scanning. **[B]**

- Important text is differentiated. (For instance, the headline is larger and "So now what?" is in bold.) **[C]**

- Overall, this helpful message is a quick read and easy to understand. **[D]**

Clearly explain what's happening

Frustrated customers don't want to waste time trying to decipher confusing or contradictory messages. Contingency design text should answer questions, not create them.

Can a visitor quickly skim the page and understand what's happening? If not, it's time to rethink your messaging.

c2it
CASH OR NO CASH?

www.c2it.com

c2it, a service for transferring cash, simultaneously informs me: **[A]** "You have no money waiting." **[B]** "You have been sent cash!" **[C]** "You currently have no cash to get." **[D]** "When you click 'Next,' the cash will be placed in your c2it Account."

So do I have money or not? This sort of dubious response is not what I want to see from a financial institution that I trust with my money. c2it must make it obvious, at a glance, whether or not I have money. Whenever possible, give visitors a single, clear message.

c2it may be using a template that doesn't take into account this sort of contingency. If your site uses template designs, make sure the templates make sense whenever visitors encounter them. Template confusion can give the impression that your site has a split personality.

As if...

Why is this bad? It's as if a bank teller is unable to give me a straight answer on whether or not I've got any money in my account.

I go online to find out whether DSL service is available for my home.

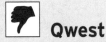 **Qwest**

www.qwest.com

> **Checking for existing service...**
> Complete
>
> **Checking Line Qualification for Service on line (303) 443-1654...**
> Complete
>
> We're sorry. Although service is available in your area, our records indicate that your telephone line does not qualify for Qwest DSL^{SM} service.
>
> We also attempted to qualify you for Qwest IDSL, an alternative high-speed Internet access solution offered by Qwest. Unfortunately your line does not qualify.

A lengthy message, entirely in boldface, appears sequentially over time and explains that although DSL service is available in my area, my telephone number does not qualify.

Overall, this is an ineffective presentation of what should be a simple message:

- Qwest trickles out the information over time and buries the most important information (that is, whether or not I can receive service) in the third paragraph.

- The entire message is written in bold, which makes it more difficult to locate the information that's actually crucial.

- The word "qualify" is presented in a different color, even though my phone line *does not* qualify.

- Qwest never explains *why* my number doesn't qualify even though "service is available in my area."

AT&T

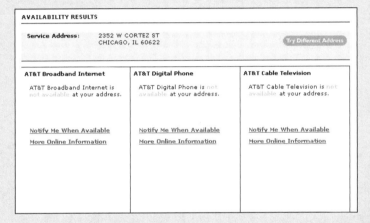

A brief message informs me that broadband service is not available at my address. The company then offers to notify me when service is made available.

AT&T shows me just the information I really need. The text is clear and brief and the most important words, "not available," are clearly highlighted with a bold typeface in a different color. In addition, AT&T's notification offer means I won't have to keep coming back to the site to check for availability.

UPS

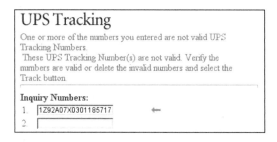

UPS Tracking

One or more of the numbers you entered are not valid UPS
Tracking Numbers.
These UPS Tracking Number(s) are not valid. Verify the
numbers are valid or delete the invalid numbers and select the
Track button.

Inquiry Numbers:
1. 1Z92A07X0301185717 ←
2.

It's tough to make heads or tails of this UPS.com error message. It twice tells me that my tracking numbers *are not* valid, yet then asks me to verify that the numbers *are* valid. Huh? Customers shouldn't have to reread an error message multiple times in order to understand it.

FedEx

SIMPLER IS BETTER   www.fedex.com

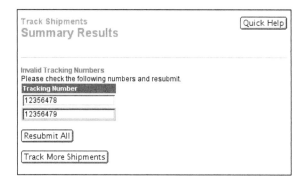

Track Shipments
Summary Results   Quick Help

Invalid Tracking Numbers
Please check the following numbers and resubmit.
Tracking Number
12356478
12356479

Resubmit All

Track More Shipments

Unlike UPS, FedEx offers a streamlined version that works much better. This brief summary is an improvement over the verbose, confusing text provided by UPS.

Still this message could be even clearer. Why not give visitors an example of a valid tracking number for comparison purposes? Also, the button language of "Resubmit All" and "Track More Shipments" is a bit confusing.

GUIDELINE 7

Be polite

Politeness is more than just good etiquette—it's good business. Upset customers need to be treated with kid gloves. So when something goes wrong at your site, be polite:

1. Don't take an accusatory tone or place blame on the customer.
2. Use words such as "please" and "thank you."
3. Don't use all caps because this can give the impression that you're screaming at customers.
4. Think rejuvenation, not condemnation.

Best Deal Magazines
WE WARNED YOU

www.bestdealmagazines.com

Duplicate Credit Card Charges: Our notice on the "Payment Information Page" of the "Shopping Cart" clearly warns that pressing on the "Order Now" button can result in duplicate credit card charges occurring and/or duplicate orders being processed. Sometimes this occurs if you double click when clicking on the Order Now button or from some glitch in your computer. In most cases this results in a duplicate order which is forwarded to the publisher and paid for by us long before the customer realizes that he/she has been double charged. We can not get a refund from the publisher even if we are able to cancel the subscription - a process which is extremely labor intensive and time consuming and not worth the effort. Therefore, in cases of such duplicate charges, we can refund only 25% of the duplicate charge but will make no effort to cancel the subscription. We recommend that you keep the two subscriptions and when you begin to receive duplicate issues of the magazine, you call the publisher and ask that the two subscriptions be combined into one two year subscription. You will get the benefit of a two year subscription for much less than our regular charge for a longer term subscription.

An incorrect credit charge is touchy business, and Best Deal Magazines isn't making any friends with this "it's not our problem" approach.

The site implies the duplicate order is my fault when it states, "Our notice…clearly warns that pressing on the 'Order Now' button can result in duplicate credit card charges…." At this point, what's the use of placing blame on the customer? The company appears to be more intent on covering its tracks than helping customers.

Even worse, the site refuses to give me a refund for the duplicate order. Then, the copywriters have the gall to recommend a head-spinning solution that involves contacting the publisher to combine magazine subscriptions. No thanks, I'll just contact my credit card company and cancel the charges.

The site could handle this situation better in several ways. Technology can be used to prevent duplicate submissions from double-clicks (see Guideline 14 in Chapter 4). Or the site could contact customers and confirm all entries submitted in close proximity to make sure double orders don't go through. Finally, if a mistake does get through, the company must take responsibility and give a refund. The solution they suggest is not realistic for most customers.

Your site's contingency design tone of voice should convey gentle assurance, like a doctor talking to a patient. Be courteous and admit your mistakes. Treating visitors with respect during sour times is crucial to your future relationship with them.

Hallmark
APOLOGETIC TONE
www.hallmark.com

Whether the problem's cause is the site or the visitor, politeness is always the right approach. When Hallmark experiences a server crunch, they go out of their way to apologize, explain the problem, and offer an alternate path to customers.

As if...

Why is this good? It's as if a kind waiter apologizes for my meal's delay and promises to bring it out the instant it's ready.

Lands' End

WE OWE IT ALL TO YOU   www.landsend.com

Contact Us Phone E-mail Fax Mailing Address

Here at Lands' End, we've always sold our products directly, so talking with customers is old hat. (And it's a rare Lands' End product that doesn't owe some improvement — or improvements — to customer feedback!) If you have a comment or suggestion, please feel free to contact us in the manner that is most convenient for you.

Having problems?
Need questions answered?
Click the Lands' End Live button to talk to us.

Customers get frustrated when a site buries contact information or discourages feedback. That's why Lands' End "contact us" tone of voice is so refreshing. The friendly copy shows that Lands' End wants my feedback and values the opinions of its customers. Also, notice how the site uses "human" language and features an image of a customer service representative. Too many online retailers sound like robots. Do all you can to humanize the interaction.

CHAPTER SUMMARY

Avoid confusing terms, technical information, and unfamiliar language when helping customers overcome crisis points. Error messages must be helpful and easy to understand for *all* visitors, even your Mom. Keep contingency design text brief and simple to ensure the message is received. Also, be courteous and never blame the customer.

Chapter Four

BULLETPROOF FORMS

Create friendly forms that are easy to complete

Guidelines covered in this chapter

8 Highlight either required or optional fields.

9 Accept entries in all common formats.

10 Provide sample entries, pull-downs, and formatting hints to ensure clean data.

11 Explicitly state limits to characters, number of entries, and so forth.

12 If customers can't choose it, don't show it.

13 Validate entries (as soon as possible).

14 Button up: Eliminate the Reset button and disable the Submit button after it's clicked.

15 Assist form dropouts by saving information.

INTRODUCTION

Forms are a hassle. "Invalid" responses, confusing choices, and unacceptable entries constantly gum up the works. It's no wonder that many busy surfers simply give up when faced with forms. Here's what you can do to help.

GUIDELINE 8

Highlight either required or optional fields

Whether it's because they are reluctant to share information online or just in a hurry (or both), many people give up on forms that ask too many questions. That's why your *forms must clearly state which fields are required and which ones are optional.* Sites often use one or more of these techniques to highlight fields:

- An asterisk (or other icon) next to the field
- The word "Required" or "Optional" next to the field
- Required field titles in boldface

Try to minimize the number of required fields whenever possible. You'll still get the information you need but you'll also let customers decide whether it's worth the time to provide extra data. If you don't identify required fields, customers may become frustrated when told that an unmarked field is actually mandatory. They may even bail out of the process completely.

Victoria's Secret

TURNED OFF

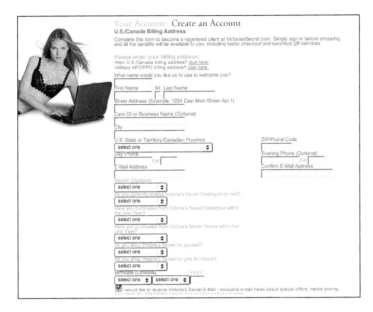

This "Create an Account" page at Victoria's Secret isn't as clear as it could be. Required fields, such as "Name" and "City," are not clearly indicated. And although some fields are tagged as optional (for instance, "Business Name" and "Evening Phone"), the site neglects to mention that the marketing questions at the end (for instance, "Do you currently receive Victoria's Secret Catalogue by mail?" and "Do you shop Victoria's Secret for yourself?") aren't actually required (you can skip them and still successfully create an account).

It would be better for the site to avoid the impression that these questions are mandatory when they're not. Otherwise, customers who don't want to share this sort of personal information may decide the process isn't worth the effort.

So how should you mark required fields? Use an asterisk or other clear icon to indicate which fields are must-haves.

Washington Post

MARKED WITH *

All fields marked with * are required.

*Name:

*Street Address:

*City: State ⬍ *Zip: 20037

*Home Phone:

Work Phone:

Email Address:

Subscription Type:

◉ 6 Months (24 weeks) of Sunday-only Delivery: $20.03

◯ 6 Months (24 weeks) of 7-day Delivery: $40.06

Continue

The Washington Post uses a red asterisk to indicate the fields that must be completed. This means customers don't have to wonder, "Can I skip this field without causing problems?"

GUIDELINE 9

Accept entries in all common formats

How do you enter a phone number? Do you use dashes, parentheses, spaces, no spaces?

How about credit cards? Do you follow the formatting on the card (with spaces) or do you write it all as one long number without spaces?

For dates, do you use dashes or slashes to separate the date? Two-character years or four-character years?

The fact is people will use different data formats at your site. That's why your forms should accept entries in all common formats. This saves customers the headache of trying to figure out which format is required.

Nordstrom

NO HYPHENS OR SPACES   www.nordstrom.com

Nordstrom's site only accepts phone numbers in this format: 2125554389. Although the site does at least offer advice on this restrictive format with its "no hyphens or spaces" message, a better solution would be to go ahead and accept all common formats. The site also should allow 212-555-4389 or 212 555 4389 or 212.555.4389.

KB Toys

IT'S ALL GOOD   www.kbtoys.com

KB Toys accepts phone numbers regardless of which entry style is chosen. That means one less barrier facing shoppers.

AOL

AUTOFORMAT   www.aol.com

AOL's signup form automatically converts phone numbers into the proper format. I entered "2125436587" and the site's form, via JavaScript, automatically translated it to (212) 543-6587 while I was typing. By automatically reformatting the number into an acceptable entry, AOL removes any possibility for formatting errors.

```
* credit card number:
6011472654872213
```

```
* credit card number:
6011 4726 5487 2213
```

Credit card numbers with or without spaces are accepted at the Zagat site. There's no need to put up an unnecessary roadblock when customers are trying to give you money.

Few things frustrate a form-filler more than being told an entry needs to conform to certain standards *after* the form is submitted. Give visitors a break by being upfront about acceptable parameters. Use sample entries, pull-downs, and formatting hints to avoid a breakdown. These tools will minimize confusion and help people quickly complete forms. This guideline will show you how to use these techniques to ensure that data is properly formatted:

- **Limit the range of entries**.
  Use HTML form elements to ensure valid submissions.

- **Give formatting examples.**
  Provide correct sample entries to prevent confusion.

- **Form guidance.**
  Use form layout to guide people in the right direction.

- **From Date** is an invalid date. Enter a valid date.

Click the **Back** button on your browser to return to the previous screen
▲ TOP OF PAGE

E*TRADE Bank, member FDIC.
Copyright © 2000 E*TRADE Bank. All rights reserved
Security and Privacy Statement

I entered "7/2/03" as a date at E*Trade, but this message informs me that this is an "invalid date." Unfortunately, E*Trade never explained the proper way to enter the date prior to entry or why the date entered was invalid (impossible date, bad format, or so on) after entry.

Even worse, E*Trade's error message *still* doesn't tell me the right format to use. Should it be 7-2-03 or 07/02/03 or something else? E*Trade's unspecific response is an invitation to additional frustration. The site should clearly indicate the proper date format to use.

Limit the range of entries

Open-ended text fields leave plenty of room for error. When given free range, visitors often wind up submitting entries that are unacceptable for one reason or another.

How can you make sure visitors stay between the lines? Pull-downs, list boxes, and check box lists can limit the range of entries to only those who you deem acceptable. These tools provide a nifty way to nudge customers in the right direction.

United Airlines

MONTH PULL-DOWN

www.united.com

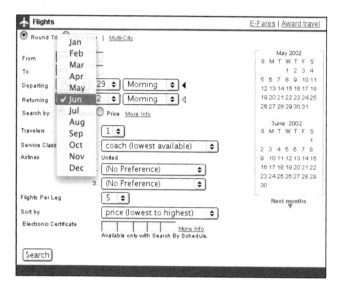

There's no way to enter an invalid date at United's site because of the pull-down menus used for date selection. This simple technique prevents mistakes and keeps visitors on track. Pull-downs are also used to ensure acceptable responses for the number of travelers, service class, flights per leg, and other fields.

DeepDiscountCD

IMPROVING THE ODDS

www.deepdiscountcds.com

DeepDiscountCDs uses pull-downs to keep credit card type, date of expiration, salutation, state, and country data accurate. This improves the odds that I will successfully complete the form on the first try.

Give formatting examples

If you don't use HTML form elements to limit entries, make sure you explicitly tell visitors the correct format to use.

Expedia and E*Trade

MM/DD/YYYY AND XXX-XX-XXXX   www.expedia.com and www.etrade.com

What date format should I use at Expedia? The hint "MM/DD/YY" makes it obvious. Should I use hyphens for my Social Security number at E*Trade? Yes, according to their format hint. Without this information, I would be forced to guess the acceptable formats.

Yahoo! and Citysearch

SAMPLE ANSWERS   weather.yahoo.com and www.citysearch.com

Yahoo! Weather and Citysearch both provide examples of proper search submissions. This lets me know what a

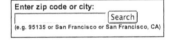

"good" entry looks like and increases the odds of a successful search.

Form guidance

Alternatively, you can also use the structure of your form to make sure people don't make mistakes.

Dell

BOXED IN   www.dell.com

What's the right way to enter a phone number at Dell? The site uses separate text boxes to eliminate any doubt. This greatly reduces the possibility of making a mistake.

GUIDELINE 11

Explicitly state limits to characters, number of entries, and so forth

Too many sites give speeding tickets without ever posting speed limit signs. If there is only a narrow range of acceptable characters or entries (for example, a text box with a limit of 20 characters or a field that allows a maximum of 10 emails), make sure you clearly explain the limit. Frustration is sure to ensue if you're not upfront about the limits visitors need to conform to in order to succeed.

Yahoo! Mail won't send my message because the "Bcc field contains too many addressees." Unfortunately, Yahoo! doesn't tell me how many addressees I *can* submit. I have to guess and guess again to get the right number. It's a frustrating process that takes too much time to figure out. Obstacles such as this make me want to find a new group mailing list provider.

As if...

Why is this bad? It's as if I try to buy 20 tickets to a sporting event but the ticket office refuses me because there is a limit on the number of tickets an individual can buy. The really frustrating part is that the ticket office won't tell me the actual limit! Instead, I have to keep guessing until I hit a number below the maximum.

A similar process occurs when a site requires a limit to the number of characters in a form field. Customers carefully word their entries, so it's essential that you communicate, at the point of entry, the allowable amount of text.

ADD A NEW ADDRESS

Please complete all fields on the form before continuing.

- Address Exceeds Maximum Allowable Length

First Name: JASON
Last Name: FRIED
Address Line 1: 37SIGNALS
Address Line 2: 314 WEST INSTITUTE
City: CHICAGO

CDNow tells me my "Address Exceeds Maximum Allowable Length" but doesn't tell me the actual maximum length I can use. As a result, I'm left with the tedious trial-and-error method as the only way to determine how much text is allowed. Plus, who uses language such as "exceeds maximum allowable length?"

From the customer...

"Another painful example of this is HotJobs.com. They have a limit on the amount of characters your resumé can contain. (They have a resumé builder tool.) This is annoying for various reasons: 1) I don't want to shorten my resumé. 2) They don't tell me how far over the limit I am when posting. I had to go through about 10 iterations before getting it right. *Annoying!*"

Your visitors need to know about these sorts of restrictions before they waste time crafting unacceptable entries. Be forthright about any limits and place this information at the point of data entry.

It's also a good idea to offer a *countdown* feature and use the "Maxlength" attribute (more to follow on this) to cap the number of characters that can be entered in the field. If customers do enter too much text, make sure you clearly explain the problem and how to fix it.

Google

25 MAX

www.google.com

Google helpfully informs me of the maximum number of characters I can enter. The site also uses the Maxlength attribute, so I'm unable to enter more than 25 characters.

Tech info

Maxlength

Use the Maxlength HTML attribute to specify the maximum number of characters a text entry box can accept. This ensures that a customer won't be able to enter too many characters. Here's an example for how to limit entries (to 50 characters in this case):

```
<input type="text" name="fieldname" maxlength="50">
```

My message is too long.

 **Paypal**

www.paypal.com

The message you have entered is too long. Please enter a shorter message.

> **Deny Payment Memo**   Secure Transact
>
> The following memo will be emailed to the sender to notify them that the payme
> has been denied. This memo will also be available in the transaction details. You
> may edit the message or leave it as is. Press "Deny" when you are done.
>
> Your money is no good here. How dare you think you can buy me
> off with just a few measley dollars. I won't have any of it. You
> don't own me, I won't sell myself for that low of a price. I'm

Paypal tells me my message is too long and asks me to enter a shorter message. Unfortunately, the site waits until *after* I submit my entry with too much text before even telling me a limit exists.

Then, the site neglects to tell me the actual limit. The only choice I have is to guess. I remove a few words and submit the text again. Still too much. I remove a few more words and try again. Still too much. Finally, I give up.

 **SprintPCS**

www.sprintpcs.com

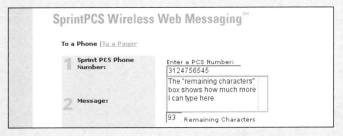

SprintPCS tells me there is a limit of 160 characters for messages. As I start typing, the number in the "Remaining Characters" box counts down to zero. When I hit the maximum, the site prevents me from entering more text and displays a JavaScript alert that says, "Maximum message length reached. Your message has been truncated at 160 characters."

What's nice is that SprintPCS is upfront about the maximum message length and clearly tells me the limit. The helpful countdown feature also gives me instant feedback on how much additional text I can type. Finally, the site stops me when I reach the text limit and tells me why. This approach prevents mistakes and keeps messaging quick and efficient.

GUIDELINE 12

If customers can't choose it, don't show it

Another way to make life easier for your customers is to eliminate unavailable options (a.k.a. prevalidation). If I can't choose an entry, don't show it to me in the first place.

Google

THEN DON'T OFFER 2003

There are errors in your submitted data.
The value of the "Ending year" field is too large. It must be at most 2002.

Start my ads running on   (MM/DD/YY):   [May ▲▼] [1] [2002 ▲▼]

Stop my ads on   (MM/DD/YY):   [Dec ▲▼] [31] [2003 ▲▼]

I'm choosing the date to stop running an ad on Google. 2003 is listed as one of the year options. (In fact, it was the default selection.) When I choose a date in 2003, however, the site informs me that 2002 is the latest year I can select.

It's frustrating to select a default option and then find out it's invalid. If I can't go past 2002, Google shouldn't even present 2003 as an option.

Ticketmaster

WHY NOT TELL ME IT'S SOLD OUT?

www.ticketmaster.com

ticketmaster

We are unable to fulfill your specific request. We may not have the type of tickets you
requested or the number of seats together that you are looking for.

If you are unable to find tickets, be sure to check back often. As the date of the event nears, many times a
limited number of tickets may be released.

©2001 Ticketmaster. All rights reserved.

I tried to buy tickets to a sold-out concert at Ticketmaster. Unfortunately, the site never actually told me the show was sold out. Instead, it displayed the show's information and let me select tickets before it actually spilled the beans that tickets for this event were *not* available.

Even then, this ambiguous error message still leaves me scratching my head. If Ticketmaster knows the event is sold out, then why not just say so? It's no wonder customers wind up ticked off at the ticket behemoth.

From the customer...

"Ticketmaster.com is a case study in how *not* to create an online service... Why can't it just tell me there are no tickets available for a particular event? Instead it keeps prompting you to try different combinations of quantity and location because you figure if it doesn't indicate that it's sold out, there must be at least one little ticket waiting to be found."

Peapod

ONLY SHOW AVAILABLE TIMES   www.peapod.com

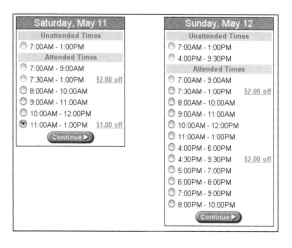

Peapod normally offers a range of delivery times throughout the day. On Saturday, however, the grocery service only has a limited number of slots available. Instead of displaying Saturday's later time slots that can't actually be chosen, *the site shows only the times that are valid selections.*

This is helpful because I don't want to select a time slot and then find out it's unavailable. By preventing this sort of wrong turn, Peapod prevents backtracking and gets me one step closer to checkout.

EasyJet

EASY PICKING   www.easyjet.com

Here, EasyJet eliminates invalid airport options. Selecting Athens as my "From" point automatically filters the options in the "To" field to display just "London Luton," the one destination available from Athens. After all, it's easyJet that knows exactly where their planes fly, not their customers.

GUIDELINE 13

Validate entries (as soon as possible)

You can improve conversion rates and make customers' lives easier by validating form responses on the spot. Check to make sure that email addresses contain an at sign (@) and no spaces, numbers are actually numbers, and other fields are filled in with acceptable responses.

AOL
NEW YORK, ALASKA?

www.aol.com

I entered an invalid email (".og" rather than ".org") along with an impossible city/state/zip combination (that is, the city is New York, the state is Alaska, and the zip code is in Illinois) at AOL's sign-up page. Yet AOL accepts all this information and allows me to continue with the sign-up process. Instead, the site should validate entries such as these to make sure that my email address is properly formatted and that the city/state/zip combo is real.

UPS
MATCH CITY AND ZIP

www.ups.com

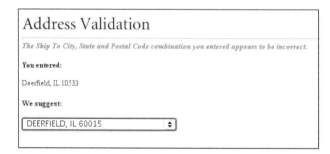

UPS knows zip code errors are a common cause of shipping mistakes. That's why they validate zip codes and make sure the city and zip match up *before* a shipment order is submitted. That way, both the customer and company come out a winner.

In this case, I accidentally entered my destination as a city in Illinois with a New York zip code. UPS catches the error and offers a pull-down menu with recommended alternatives (including appropriate matches for both the city and zip code I entered).

Most sites don't validate addresses on the spot, meaning this sort of error isn't caught until it's too late. UPS's smart validating saves me time and keeps my shipment on track.

As if...

Why is this good? It's as if I'm buying new tires for my car. I pick out a set, but the salesclerk informs me that this particular set won't fit my car. He then shows me another set of tires that will fit.

Motley Fool
ENTER A VALID NUMBER

www.fool.com

The Motley Fool site spots an improperly formatted phone number right away. This message explains the proper format for the entry. The site could go a step further and provide an example, too.

NBA
INVALID EMAIL

www.nba.com

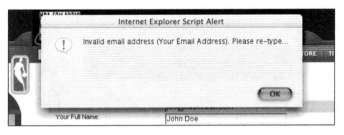

The NBA site gives an alert that the email field is not completed properly. (It was left blank.) Friendlier language could be used, however. A better message would read, "You didn't enter a valid email address (for example: shaq_oneil@lalakers.com). Please try again."

Tech info

Validation scripts
Online resources offer free cut-and-paste JavaScript examples to use at your site. For example, The JavaScript Source (http://javascript.internet.com) offers a handy email address validation script that makes sure people don't enter multiple at signs (@s) or continuous dots (.s) in the address (for instance, james@@hotmail.com and susan@bbc..co.uk).

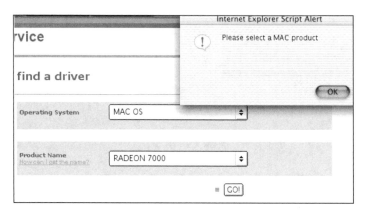

I went to download a driver at ATI. I selected "Mac OS" as my operating system, but then mistakenly chose a non-Mac product. Thankfully, ATI checks to make sure that the OS and product are compatible. The site spots the error and informs me that I need to select a Mac product before moving on. This saves me time and frustration.

Tech info

Server-side validation

Keep in mind that server-side validation is the only *fail-safe* method for error checking. JavaScript is helpful because it can be used to validate forms quickly (no time-consuming server trip is required) but can be problematic as a standalone solution because some people's browsers may have it disabled. An ideal solution is to offer both: JavaScript as the first line of defense and a server-side check as the backup.

Overvalidation

Don't overvalidate forms, however. If you have international visitors, you may have to account for country-specific data (for instance, no zip code, an international phone number with a plus sign [+] at the beginning, and so on). You want to make sure you don't shut down these visitors with excessive validation techniques. In some cases, you may want to allow visitors to override error messages and submit the data as is.

When it comes to buttons, one wrong click can ruin an otherwise successful form experience. Inadvertently clicking Reset can delete an entire form's data. Accidentally double-click Submit and you may wind up submitting information twice (resulting in multiple accounts, purchases, or some other unintended consequence).

People rushing through forms don't carefully read explanatory text or buttons before submitting a form and often make one of these mistakes. Make sure this sort of misclick isn't a deal breaker.

Eliminate reset buttons

Reset buttons (a.k.a. Clear or Cancel) are an invitation to frustration. These buttons are rarely useful and pose a dangerous threat to visitors who are trying to complete forms: One wrong click and all that labor-intensive data entry is lost. Reset buttons also increase confusion because they force people to process the impact of different buttons to determine the proper next step.

There isn't much benefit to Reset buttons. Visitors can easily use the browser's Refresh button to clear form information or just type over the existing data. So when it comes to Reset buttons, just say no.

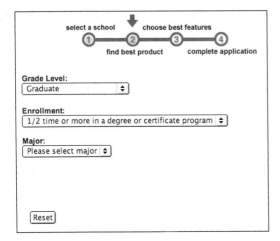

Bank One's student loan application features one button at the bottom of the screen. Clicking that button will submit my information and take me to the next step of the process, right? Actually, no. The one button displayed is Reset—one click and all the data on this page is erased.

It turns out the Continue to Step 3 button appears only after the final pull-down option is selected. Bank One would be doing its customers a service by eliminating the Reset button altogether and showing the Continue to Step 3 button as disabled until all necessary conditions are met.

Credit Card Type:	Choose a credit card type
Credit Card Number:	
	Credit card information is required to apply online. If you would prefer to print and mail in your application, please click here
Credit Card Exp. Date:	(MM/YYYY)
Credit Card CVV or CID Code:	Click here for explanation
Please answer the following questions:	How many letters and small parcels do you ship using domestic OVERNIGHT delivery service? /month
	How many letters and small parcels do you ship using domestic NON-OVERNIGHT delivery service? /month
	How many packages do you ship internationally? /month

[Send Request] [Clear Fields]

Here, FedEx makes a mistake by placing a Clear Fields button adjacent to the Send Request button. The Clear Fields button adds confusion and will cause problems when visitors in a hurry click it by mistake. How often is someone going to want to delete *everything* he just typed anyway? Just because the site can include a Clear button doesn't mean it should.

Confirm deletions

In the rare instance that a form does require a Clear or Reset button, try to confirm the action to minimize the chance that a visitor deletes data accidentally.

University of Washington

ARE YOU SURE?   www.washington.edu

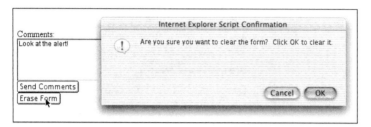

I clicked the Erase Form button on this page at the University of Washington's site. The site uses a JavaScript alert to confirm my intentions. It's always a good idea to confirm data deletion to prevent the dreaded "Where'd all my info go!?"

Disable submit button once pressed

Too many sites scare customers with this sort of tough button talk:

"Click the Order button *one time only* and then wait for your order to process. If you click the button more than once, you will be charged for multiple orders!"

Ominous language and false charges? Not the way to make friends online.

Whether on purpose or by accident, customers will sometimes wind up double-clicking form buttons. There is a way to prevent duplicate submissions, however. *Use JavaScript to disable buttons once they are clicked*. Then, the script can change the button (for instance, fade it out to show it's been pressed and/or present new text that explains the situation, such as "Please wait while we process your order").

E*Trade

CLICK ONLY ONCE   www.etrade.com

Creating a new account at E*Trade? Hopefully you're not trigger-happy. After you click Continue, you'll have to wait up to a minute for your entry to process. And if you mistakenly click the button twice (or click Stop and then click Continue), you'll end up with multiple accounts. E*Trade could prevent this messy scenario by disabling the button after it's clicked and changing the text to "Processing, please wait. This may take up to a minute." Alternatively, the site could provide an intermediate status page between the submission of the form and the results page.

Applied Biosystems

DISABLING A BUTTON   www.appliedbiosystems.com

Language	English ♦
Researcher Name	
Researcher Phone	
Contact Person	

☐ I would like to receive information pertaining to the Applied Biosystems e-commerce store.

☐ Please do not show sequence information on the order confirmation, packing slips or invoices.

[Continue]

Language	English ♦
Researcher Name	
Researcher Phone	
Contact Person	

☐ I would like to receive information pertaining to the Applied Biosystems e-commerce store.

☐ Please do not show sequence information on the order confirmation, packing slips or invoices.

[Wait]

Applied Biosystems realizes customers may click a button more than once. To prevent duplicate submissions, the site uses JavaScript to disable the button after it's pressed. The code also changes the button's value from Continue (the button's original state) to Wait (the disabled state) so that visitors know what's happening. It's a nifty solution to a common problem.

Let's say I'm in the middle of filling out a lengthy registration form and my browser crashes. Or maybe I'm completing a gift purchase but realize I don't have the recipient's address on me. Or perhaps I'm late for dinner and don't have time to complete an account profile.

In any of these situations, I'll be forced to bail out and return to the site in question. When I come back, will I have to start from scratch or will my information be saved? The answer may be the difference between a lost customer and a satisfied one.

Just because a visitor abandons a form, it doesn't necessarily mean he or she won't come back to complete it later. Your site can help visitors like this get back in the saddle by saving data as it is entered. It's a great way to make an application, registration, or checkout process easier to complete. Customers will appreciate your proactive efforts and conversion rates will increase if you follow these measures:

1. **Save customer data.**
   Automatically save in-progress forms (or let visitors choose to save this data).

2. **Tell form-fillers the data is saved.**
   Use your site or email to remind visitors that they can easily jump back into an abandoned form process.

3. **Provide easy access.**
   Enable people to quickly access and complete abandoned forms.

What are the real-world applications of this technique? You can hold items in a customer's shopping cart so that they can be purchased later. Or store sign-up information so a customer doesn't need to start over from scratch. Or save a mortgage application when the applicant doesn't have all the required information at that moment.

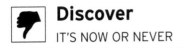

Discover
IT'S NOW OR NEVER

www.discoverhomeloans.com

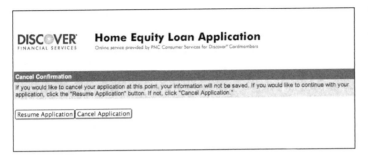

While filling out a home equity loan application at Discover, I realized that I did not have all the information I needed (that is, I didn't know the total square footage of my property).

Unfortunately, Discover doesn't let me save the other information I've entered successfully, meaning I'll have to re-enter it all again. Discover should allow me to save this application so that later I can pick up where I left off.

Bank One
SAVING FOR LATER

www.bankone.com

Bank One realizes lengthy loan applications can be difficult to complete in one sitting. That's why the site lets student loan applicants save applications and retrieve them later.

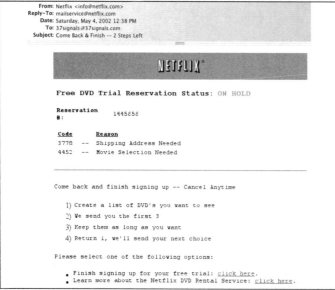

I abandoned the Netflix free-trial sign-up process at the final stage because I wanted to browse the video selection library more. The site wisely offers a persistent "Finish Sign-Up" link at the top of each page as I browse the rest of the site. This way I'm never more than one click away from returning to where I left off in the sign-up process.

After I leave the site, Netflix even goes a step further by sending an email to let me know my information is saved. The message also notifies me of the information that's still needed to complete the process. The email closes with a helpful link to "Finish signing up for your free trial." Tactics such as this are part of the reason Netflix recently doubled its subscription base in less than a year.

As if...

My computer crashes, but the application I'm working in autosaves the open documents so that I don't have to start from the beginning again.

CHAPTER SUMMARY

Effective form contingency design is a great way to boost conversion rates. Highlight required fields so that people know which ones are optional. Customers don't want to guess at acceptable entry types, so make sure you accept entries in all commonly used formats. Also, provide examples, pull-downs, and formatting hints to prevent data entry miscues. If there are limits on certain form fields, be upfront about them so that visitors don't wind up frustrated later on. Prevent bad data from entering the system by eliminating unacceptable options and validating entries on the spot. Eliminate button confusion by omitting Reset buttons and disabling Submit buttons after they're clicked. Finally, let people save lengthy forms so that they can complete them later.

Chapter Five

MISSING IN ACTION
Overcome missing pages, images, or plug-ins

Guidelines covered in this chapter

16 Offer customized "Page Not Found" error pages

17 Successfully redirect near-miss URLs

18 Use ALT tags for images

19 Offer alternative pages or upgrade info for old browsers

INTRODUCTION

Is your site sometimes missing in action? No matter how hard you try to create the perfect browsing experience, visitors will sometimes wind up facing missing information.

The most usable screen is worthless if a customer mistypes a URL and never gets there. Smart-looking navigation images don't matter if they don't actually load on a visitor's browser. Nifty plug-ins become black holes if they prevent someone from entering your site.

Your site needs to have a better response than "it's not our fault" to problems such as these. Intervene and help customers overcome botched URLs, old browsers, server issues, and other M.I.A. problems that may leave visitors out in the cold. Here's how.

Whether it's because of an outdated link, a typo, a restricted directory, or a server malfunction, customers frequently request a URL that is not available. Design a customized "Page Not Found" screen that explains the situation and helps visitors get to the information they're looking for.

Too many web sites never bother to change the default "404" error message provided by their web servers. These nondescript screens are confusing and do little to aid customers at a time when they clearly need help. It's no wonder many visitors abandon sites when faced with these unhelpful pages.

 **Home Depot**
WHERE'S THE BEEF?

Not Found

The requested object does not exist on this server. The link you followed is either outdated, inaccurate, or the server has been instructed not to let you have it.

I entered a bad URL at Home Depot's site, and this is the screen I see. What's a "requested object"? Why can't I click to another page? An unhelpful default "404" message such as this just doesn't cut it. This amateurish "Page Not Found" is inappropriate for a major retailer such as Home Depot.

Instead of merely saying a page is not found, your site needs to explain why a page can't be located and offer suggestions for getting to the right screen. Your site should lend a hand, not kick people when they are down.

Smart things to include on your 404 page:

1. Your company's name and logo
2. An explanation of why the visitor is seeing this page
3. A list of common mistakes that may explain the problem
4. Links back to the home page and/or other pages that might be relevant
5. A search engine that customers can use to find the right information
6. An email link so that visitors can report problems, missing pages, and so on

Apple

TOP-NOTCH 404

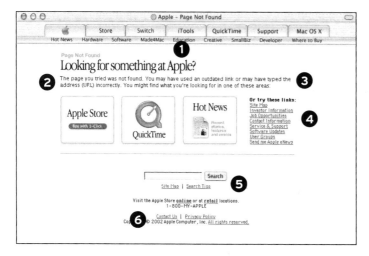

Apple's "Page Not Found" screen displays all the features a good 404 page should have. It contains the following:

1. The company name and logo

2. An explanation that the requested page cannot be found

3. Some possible reasons for the failure

4. A standard navigation bar and links to the most requested pages at the site

5. A search engine (as well as links to a site map and search help)

6. A "Contact Us" link

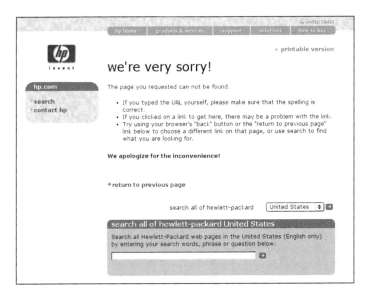

In this example, HP does a good job of explaining why the requested page can't be found. Also note the courteous, apologetic tone. HP realizes that politeness is crucial at a crisis point like this (see Guideline 7 in Chapter 3).

Tech info

Finding bad links

Check your server's referral log pages to see which page is sending visitors to a broken link at your site. If the bad link is on your own site, go ahead and fix it. If the link is at an external site, contact the site owner to correct the problem. Although visitors will sometimes report outdated or incorrect links, don't rely on this as your sole discovery tactic.

I enter a URL for a page that no longer exists on the site.

 **Moviefone**

www.moviefone.com

> **Not Found**
>
> The requested URL was not found on this server.
>
> AOLserver/3.3pre on http://www.moviefone.com
>
> ..

Moviefone presents me with a generic "Not Found" screen. The brief message ("The requested URL was not found on this server") does nothing to help me get back on track. And where is the company's name and logo? Links to other pages? Search engine? Contact information? This page leaves me dazed and confused.

IBM

www.ibm.com

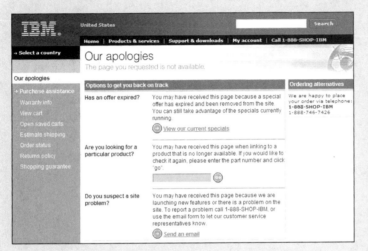

IBM presents me with an apology and gives me two options for finding the page I want. The site also provides a phone number and an email link to report the problem. By providing site navigation as well as multiple avenues to help customers, IBM is doing all that it can to get visitors back on track. The feedback options also send a clear message that IBM is a customer-focused company that cares about getting things right.

Help Center

The New York Times
ON THE WEB

| Home | Site Index | Site Search | Forums | Archives | Marketplace |

Page Not Found

The page you've requested does not exist at this address. Please note:

- If you typed in the address, used a bookmark, or followed a link from another Web site: the page is no longer available, since most articles remain online for only one week following the day of publication. Articles back to 1996 are available in our Archive (text-only), which you can search below. Searching and summaries are free; the full text of archive articles can be purchased with these pricing options: 25 articles for $19.95, 10 articles for $9.95, four articles for $5.50, or single articles for $2.50 each.

SEARCH THE SITE

[   ] [Past 30 Days ⇕] [Search]

- E-Mail Update readers: If the article links in your mailing do not work, your e-mail program may not support the HTML version of the mailings. Please switch to the Text Version.

- Because the AP/Reuters newswires are updated so frequently, you will sometimes get this error if you connect to an AP page at the moment that it is updated. Click your browser's Back button and then then Refresh to try again.

- If you clicked on a headline or other link on NYTimes.com, you can report the missing page.

This in-depth "Page Not Found" screen at The New York Times explains the possible causes for the error and offers multiple resolution paths for readers. The screen also includes navigation links, a search engine, and a feedback link to report the missing page. The page would be easier to scan if the site were to shorten the text and use headlines for each bulleted paragraph.

GUIDELINE 17

Successfully redirect near-miss URLs

Customers won't always enter URLs exactly right. Sometimes they'll guess incorrectly at a domain name. Other times, they may slightly misspell a URL. These minor errors can mean a lost visitor and a blown opportunity. If it's a URL mistake that occurs often, intervene and redirect surfers to the proper page.

How can you help these "close but no cigar" visitors get to the right page? Overcome URL confusion by accepting common misspellings, typos, incorrect case sensitivity, abbreviations, or other predictable domain name errors.

I typed "www.apple.com/iTunes" in my browser's address bar but instead of information on the MP3 application, I received a "Page Not Found" error. Even though the actual name of the app is "iTunes," Apple's site only accepts "www.apple.com/itunes" (all lowercase).

This is an unfortunate branding situation for Apple. Customers are actually punished for adhering to the brand's naming conventions!

Apple needs to adjust its server software to overcome case sensitivity, especially for pages related to products such as iTunes and iPod. Sites should always relax or eliminate case sensitivity in URLs to be as flexible as possible.

As if...

Why is this bad? It's as if I get thrown out of a French restaurant because I incorrectly pronounce the name of a dish.

Excite

ONE TOO MANY

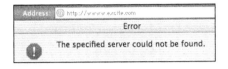

In a rush, I quickly typed in Excite's URL as "wwww.excite.com" (with too many "w"s). Unlike other sites that plan for this contingency, Excite isn't set up to handle this request. The result is a "Server Not Found" message.

Amazon

ONE TOO FEW "W"S

Amazon realizes that it's not unusual for customers to enter too few or too many "w"s in a web address. Here, I typed only two "w"s in the URL, yet I'm still properly directed to Amazon's home page.

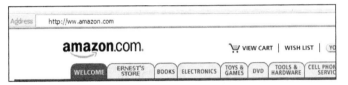

As if...

Why is this good? It's as if I send a letter to a friend but forget to include the zip code. Despite this mistake, the post office recognizes the address and delivers the letter to the proper recipient.

Tech info

Subdomain wildcards

Set up your web servers with a subdomain wildcard (*) so that any "*.yourdomain.com" will redirect visitors to your home page. Visitors will get to the right page even if they type one "w," four "w"s, press another key, or guess incorrectly at a subdomain.

Google

OOO YEAH

www.google.com

You can see another example of helpful URL guidance at Google. The company's unique name is essential to its brand identity, but it's also a bit confusing to newbies. That's why Google makes sure that customers wind up at the right page, even if they type in too many "o"s. Enter "www.gooogle.com" and you'll still wind up at Google's home page.

Other sites with potentially confusing names also take the same approach. You'll get to Victoria's Secret home page even if you type "www.victoriasecret.com" with one "s." The *Chicago Sun-Times* accepts both "www.suntimes.com" and "www.sun-times.com." SF.citysearch.com redirects to bayarea.citysearch.com. Are there common "off" URLs that you should redirect at your site?

Yahoo!

PHOTO OR PHOTOS?

photos.yahoo.com

I went to check the photo collection that I posted a while back at Yahoo!'s photo section. My hazy memory recalls photo.yahoo.com as the URL for the photo area, so I type that into my browser's address bar. Although I'm incorrect (it's actually photos.yahoo.com with an "s"), Yahoo informs me of the correct address and offers a link to the correct page. This technique clearly points out the mistake so that visitors don't repeat the error in the future.

GUIDELINE 18

Use ALT tags for images

Use ALT tags to describe your site's images and their functions. If you don't, visitors will be forced to wait for the images to download before they can take action.

Who cares about ALT tags?

- **Visitors with slow connections**
  Do 56Kbps surfers really want to wait for all your images to load?
- **Visitors who have images turned off**
  Will they still be able to navigate your site?
- **Visually impaired visitors**
  Does your site become useless without images?
- **Search engines**
  Most search engines can't crawl and index text that is image based.

These groups will appreciate text backups that describe the images on the screen. Using ALT tags will also improve your ranking in many search engines.

Tech info

ALT tags
ALT tags are the words that are displayed before an image loads (or instead of an image if graphics are disabled or don't load). They are easy to add to your HTML code. Here's an example:

`<IMG WIDTH=170 HEIGHT=125 BORDER=0 ALT="This is the text that will show up in place of the image." SRC="image.gif">`

J. Crew
NO ALTERNATIVE

www.jcrew.com

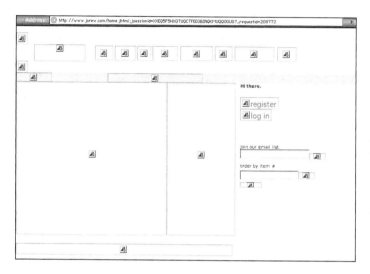

J. Crew's image-heavy home page doesn't degrade gracefully. With images turned off, the navigation and other graphics on the page are worthless. At least the site offers ALT tags for "register" and "login." Why not include explanatory text for the other images, too?

Red Envelope
MISSING NAVIGATION

www.redenvelope.com

Red Envelope has a similar problem. In this case, some of the images on the page load, whereas others don't. If the site used ALT tags for the navigation images, I would still be able to click through to the appropriate sections. Unfortunately, I can only guess what the other sections are besides "Occasion" and "Recipient."

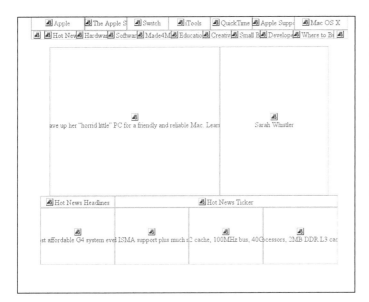

Apple wisely uses ALT tags to back up the site's image-heavy home page. That way a server crunch does not destroy the customer experience. Despite the slow load time, I can still see what's on the page and click through to my desired area of the site.

As if...

Why is this good? It's as if I want to watch an interview on television but the audio isn't working. I turn on closed-captioning so that I can at least read what is being said.

Not all potential customers will have the most recent browser or plug-in technology. Instead of merely rejecting these visitors, offer an alternative version of your content so that these potential customers aren't shut out.

If you can't offer redundant versions of your content, make sure to explain the technology issue and offer links to the proper upgrades.

Also, ask yourself whether bleeding-edge technology is even necessary at your site. It's unwise to force visitors to upgrade their browser or download a plug-in unless there's a compelling reason to do so.

Warren Center

SIMPLER IS BETTER

www.warrencenter.com

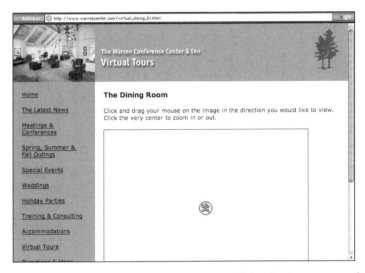

This virtual tour at the Warren Conference Center site requires a special plug-in from iPix. Because I don't have the required plug-in, I see a broken link box rather than the virtual tour of the center's dining room. The page fails to offer a link to the plug-in. Although a link to iPix is located on the virtual tour index page, shouldn't there also be one here? Also, why not include a link to the static images of the dining room, which are located elsewhere on the site?

Versace

HAVE IT YOUR WAY

www.versace.com

Versace offers a non-Flash version of its site for visitors who are unable to view the Flash version. Whenever possible, offer an alternative version of content that is viewable to all visitors. Also, the site should consider adding a link to download the Flash plug-in.

Connected Earth
PLUG-IN BREAKDOWN

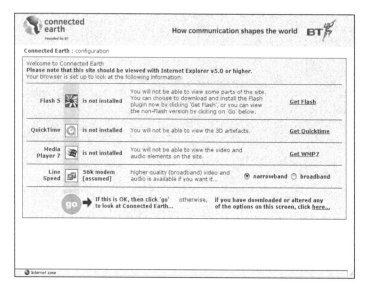

It's best if your site doesn't shut out visitors who are missing certain technologies. However, what if your site requires them? Connected Earth shows how to offer a clear explanation of the situation. Connected Earth informs visitors of browser plug-ins that are not installed, the impact each one will have on how the site is viewed, and where to download the tools.

Sumomusic
FLASH HELP

Sumomusic offers a concise, effective message to customers who don't have the Flash plug-in needed to view the site.

In an ideal situation, the site would also offer a non-Flash version to ensure access to the site for all visitors.

Yellow Pencil

IT WORKS, BUT PLEASE UPGRADE

> **Please note:** This site's design is only visible in a graphical browser that supports Web standards, but its content is accessible to any browser or Internet device. To see this site as it was designed please upgrade to a Web standards compliant browser.

Yellow Pencil offers this message to viewers who are unable to view their Cascading Style Sheets (CSS)-based layout properly. Note that the site's content is still available, it's just not properly formatted.

Upgrade messages are always a good idea for surfers with old browsers. If visitors can't view your site due to outdated software on their system, inform them and offer a link to the proper upgrade.

CHAPTER SUMMARY

Design a customized "Page Not Found" screen that explains what's wrong and helps visitors get to the right page. Overcome URL confusion by accepting common misspellings, typos, incorrect case sensitivity, abbreviations, or other predictable domain name errors. Use ALT tags to describe your site's images and their functions. Always offer an alternative version of your content so that visitors aren't shut out. If necessary, explain any site limitations due to client-side technology and offer links to software that can solve the problem.

Chapter Six

LEND A HELPING HAND

Offer help that's actually helpful

Guidelines covered in this chapter

20   Answer questions on the same page they arise.

21   Offer a "Help" section and provide clear links
     to it.

22   Let customers help themselves through online
     forums and training sessions.

23   Provide a fallback plan (help via chat, phone,
     or email).

24   Respond to emails quickly and effectively.

25   Help login with tips or email.

INTRODUCTION

A site's "Help" section may not seem as sexy as the home page or checkout process, but it's often just as important. When visitors are frustrated, they turn to help content to resolve issues and get questions answered. This information needs to be delivered swiftly and accurately to save frustrated visitors.

Here are the keys to giving visitors quick, easy access to the help and FAQ (frequently asked questions) information they need.

GUIDELINE 20

Answer questions on the same page they arise

Minimize clicks and save customers time by offering contextual help, which provides instructions and answers as close to the potential problem spot as possible.

The benefit of contextual help is that visitors don't have to leave a page (or process) to find answers elsewhere on your site. Instead, issues are solved on the spot and visitors keep headed toward their goal.

So if a term or acronym is puzzling, define it right there. Is a shipping policy perplexing customers? Clarify it during the checkout process instead of forcing visitors to leave and get help somewhere else on your site.

Wedding Channel
SANITY SAVERS

www.weddingchannel.com

Wedding Channel offers a feature called "Sanity Savers." But will future brides and grooms really understand what this link means? The site should anticipate visitor confusion at this point and offer an explanation. For example, the site could say, "Sanity Savers (Q&A with our experts who reveal sanity-saving solutions to common wedding woes)." Or the site could avoid this ambiguous lingo altogether (see Guideline 5) and use more straightforward language.

Lands' End
ON-THE-SPOT HELP

www.landsend.com

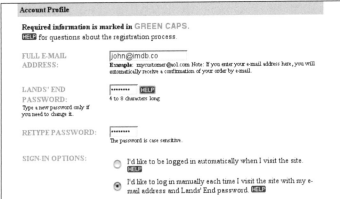

Lands' End offers a clear help link adjacent to each potentially confusing field at the site's "Account Profile" page. In this case, the "Sign-In Options" confused me (should I choose to log in manually or automatically?), so I clicked on one of the help links next to the field's options. A pop-up window appeared that explained the options and then offered a link back to the area in question.

Yahoo!

CONTEXTUAL HELP   www.yahoo.com

Verify your Yahoo! password to continue.

Return to Yahoo!
Yahoo! ID: mlinderman
Password: [   ]
[Continue]
Mode: Standard | Secure

Sign in as a different user

Why am I being asked for my password?

- To protect your account, you need to confirm your password periodically. (more)
- Only one account can be signed in at a time. If you're not "mlinderman", sign in with your own ID.

Member Details

Birthdate: *Not displayed for security reasons*
Gender: [male ▲▼]
Industry: [Select Industry] ▲▼
Title: [Select a Title] ▲▼
Specialization: [Select a Specialization] ▲▼

Why?
Your member details are used to better personalize Yahoo!'s services.

Email Information

Select Primary Alternate Email Address:
Yahoo Mail: mlinderman@yahoo.com
◉ Alternate Email 1: [josh@imdb.com]
  Non-verified
○ Alternate Email 2: [   ]
  Non-verified
○ Alternate Email 3: [   ]
  Non-verified
○ Alternate Email 4: [   ]

Why?
Password changes and account confirmations are sent to your alternate email. If you choose, Yahoo! can send special offers to your email too.

General Preferences

Time Zone: [U.S. Central   ▲▼]
Language & Content: [English – United States ▲▼]
Prompt for Password: [Every Day ▲▼]

Why?
These general settings control how Yahoo! displays your personalized information.

Smart companies integrate help FAQs throughout their sites as a preemptive strike against confusion. Here are two examples of this technique at Yahoo! In the first example, Yahoo! anticipates my frustration at being forced to re-enter my password. Instead of making me hunt for the reason for this prompt, Yahoo! explains the issue on the spot.

Yahoo! also realizes that customers are concerned about the privacy of their personal data. In the second screen, Yahoo! goes out of its way to explain exactly why each piece of information is needed in order to assuage the concerns of anxious customers.

Amazon's home page stated "Free shipping on orders over $50" but my $50+ order still included a shipping charge. Why? Amazon offers an explanatory link right next to the order information so that I can find out. It turns out that I didn't select the correct shipping method. I quickly corrected the problem and completed my transaction without the shipping charge. If Amazon wants to reach out to customers even more, the site should make the free shipping option the default selection.

GUIDELINE 21

Offer an easy-to-use "Help" section and provide clear links to it

Although you should strive to answer questions on the same screen they arise (Guideline 20), this won't always be enough. That's why you need to offer a clearly marked "Help" area to aid confused visitors. Visitors have been trained to seek "Help" when things go wrong. Don't disappoint them. Here are some guidelines:

- **"Help" should be an obvious link from your home page and in the main navigation area on all pages.**
  This way, visitors can easily get answers from any screen. Help should always be easy to reach; the same way 911 is easy to dial, your "Help" needs to be a quick click away when a web emergency occurs.

- **Use a standard naming convention for the link.**
  "Help" is usually the best choice, although you may want to use something like "Customer Service," "FAQs," or "Tips and Tricks" if it is more appropriate for your content. Just make sure the title used is obvious to your visitors. If you force them to hunt for help, they'll often just give up.

- **Organize your help section wisely.**
  If your site contains a large amount of help content, make sure it's easy to get to the right piece of information.

Any sizeable "Help" or "FAQ" section should…

- **Offer "Help" search functionality.**
  Let visitors search for keywords instead of forcing them to browse through lengthy text or long link lists.

- **Emphasize top issues.**
  If 80 percent of your customers seek help to the same 5 questions, highlight those questions so that they're easy to find.

- **Break down content into categories.**
  An avalanche of questions or links can be intimidating; use categories to make scanning easier.

- **Provide a contact link for further assistance.**
  Let customers contact you directly if they can't find what they're looking for.

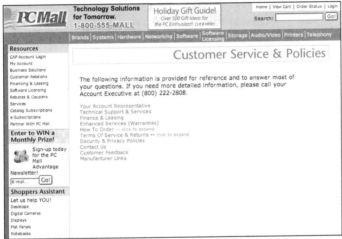

I'm having problems with an item I ordered from PC Mall but where do I turn? The site's home page features tons of links, but none of them are called "Help." Finally, I try the "Customer Relations" link located in the Resources list on the left side. PC Mall should really put this link in the main navigation bar and call it "Help" rather than "Customer Relations" (a term that resonates with business executives more than average customers).

The "Customer Relations" link actually takes me to a page called "Customer Service & Policies" (note the inconsistent naming) that gives a list of help links. This screen would be more helpful if it offered a "Help" search and mentioned some of the most common issues upfront. The site does provide an 800 number for customers, however.

eBay's help comes in the form of this bare-bones pop-up window. Many buyers and sellers probably miss out on the help they need because the site doesn't offer a "Help"-specific search, call out top FAQs, or offer contact information. At least the screen does break down the content into categories that expand to reveal subtopics when clicked.

Yahoo! Chat

HELP THAT'S ACTUALLY HELPFUL   www.yahoo.com

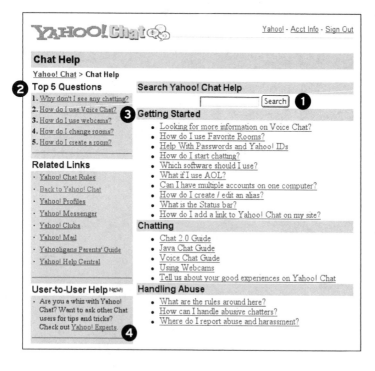

Yahoo!'s Chat Help is well designed. Note how the screen offers

1. A search engine limited to chat help content.

2. The top five questions asked by visitors.

3. Category "chunks" for easy scanning.

4. A link to get help from "Yahoo! Experts."

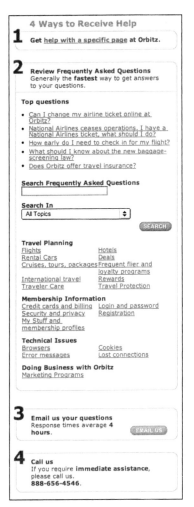

The Orbitz "Help" section is a great example to follow. Four discrete "Help" sections provide you with multiple resolution paths. Visitors can get help with a specific page, review FAQs (with the top questions highlighted on this screen), search FAQs, or go to a specific help category (for instance, "Travel Protection" or "Error Messages"). Customers also can email or call for assistance. Orbitz even mentions the average response time for email inquiries, a nice touch.

Amazon

NEED FURTHER ASSISTANCE?

www.amazon.com

Need further assistance? Click the button to E-mail us .

Did this help? Continue shopping.

Still have questions? Search help or contact us.

I finished reading an Amazon help page but still had an unanswered question. Thankfully, Amazon offers other help paths at the end of each support page, a logical spot for this information. This means that if unanswered questions linger, customers can quickly email a service representative or search "Help."

GUIDELINE 22

Let customers help themselves through online forums and training sessions

Self-help options such as community help boards and online training sessions can be a great resource for customers. (Community support boards aren't a free ride, however. Your staff will need to monitor them to control rumors, slander, spamming, and inaccurate information.) These tools let people find answers on their own and lighten your support staff's workload. Although these methods won't replace your "Help" section, they can be another effective way to reach out to people in trouble.

Blogger

BLOGGER SUPPORT CENTER

Welcome to the Blogger Support Center. Please browse our list of common articles/questions or use one of our other resources below.

Blogger Basics

- Getting Started With Blogger
- Disapearing Archives
- How do I add my own web and email links to my template?
- Is there a way to change the name that appears on my blog?

Blog*Spot Plus

- Before You Upgrade
- Getting Started Guide
- How To Upload
- Where's my upload button?

Blogger Pro

- Pro Features
- Blogger Pro FAQ
- Does One subscription cover all my blogs?

The blogging community is a tightknit one. Blogger, the tool used by many weblog authors, should use this to its advantage and let customers help each other overcome difficulties. Unfortunately, it doesn't. A message board that lets visitors post and answer questions could help them solve many problems on their own.

What are the advantages to community help boards and other third-party forums?

- They give customers instant access to answers.

- They are available 24/7.

- Once set up, they practically run themselves. This means your own customers take care of some of your heavy lifting.

- Customers like the open, unfettered dialogue they allow.

- Companies can monitor discussions to figure out soft spots at sites and stop future problems.

eBay offers community help boards where buyers and sellers can solicit answers and read previous Q&A threads. Adobe lets customers participate in "User to User Forums" dedicated to the company's different software products. Adobe also offers online training sessions and tutorials so that customers can learn on their own. This do-it-yourself approach is a great supplement to full-serve help.

Related Links

- Find your answer immediately via Community Help boards.
- Contact Customer Support.

Welcome to the Technical Issues Discussion Board! This board is for eBay members to learn more about the hardware and software that is used to trade on eBay from other community members with the support of eBay staff. If you are not an eBay registered user, please register here first - it's fast and free! Otherwise, click below to start a discussion or enter an existing thread. Prior to posting, please read and familiarize yourself with the eBay Board Usage Policies. New to eBay's discussion boards? Click here for a quick tutorial.

List of Topics
- indicates new discussions.
- indicates updated discussions.
- indicates updated by eBay Staff.

More **To Last** (903 following items)

Updated	Replies	Topic (Started by)
Nov 4	0	Please read this regarding the script errors on search results pages (randys@ebay.com)
Dec 5	4	Frustrated with Ebay's Help System (bethanyrussell)
Dec 5	2	ebay listings not showing (tbirdtim55)
Dec 5	3208	GREAT PRESENT HUNT (thump13@webtv.net)
Dec 5	1	Anyone experienced with the KLEV virus / worm? (cctv2000)
Dec 5	0	Andale counters in eBay store not working (lesliev)
Dec 5	1	Virus detected downloading turbo lister (rmatl@worldnet.att.net)
Dec 5	1	Multiple listings of the same Item (photoman62)
Dec 5	3	"Add to favorites" a Stores-Only Link? Why not all Sellers? (mittensandboots)
Dec 5	4	Not receiving notification emails. (demandred_bolt)
Dec 5	2	Dutch Auction Question - Ebay Glitch??? (baskets-of-buttons)
Dec 5	2	HELP - When I did a search for my item it did not show up in the mix. (telegrahams@earthlink.net)
Dec 5	5	POP-UPS killing your rebids??? OPT OUT!! (kathryn)

Training
Learn from self-paced online lessons, books, videos, certified training providers, events, and seminars that will help you get the most from your Adobe products.

User to User Forums
Share your Adobe product questions and experiences with other Adobe users.

---

user to user forums

You have **guest access** to browse. To post a message or add a topic, you must login or register.

read subscriptions   message center   search   preferences   login   help

Topic

Best location for scratch disk with single partitioned HD?

Stanley Katz - 01:40pm Dec 5, 2002 Pacific

For the next several months I'm constrained to using a laptop --XP Pro with a single 60GB HD which will be partitioned using PartitionMagic.

Is there any concensus as to whether or not, in that case, it is better to locate the PS7 scratch disk in its own partition separate from the OS/win swap file, and the PS7 files?

Stan Katz

As if...

Why is this good? It's as if my car is making a strange noise. I'm about to take it to the mechanic when a car-savvy friend tells me a simple solution that solves the problem. The quick fix saves me a visit to the service station.

GUIDELINE 23

Provide a human fallback plan (help via chat, phone, or email)

If customers can't find the help information they need at your site, make sure you *offer links to email, telephone, live chat, or other support options.*

Many sites turn people off by burying the company's contact information. It's as if they'd rather not deal with those pesky customers who actually want to talk with a real human being rather than a computer.

Show customers that you care by going out of your way to solicit customer feedback and offer help. After all, you want potential customers to complete transactions, not waste time searching for your contact information. Plus, customer feedback can often reveal hard-to-find problem spots.

eBay
SNAIL-MAIL HELP?

www.ebay.com

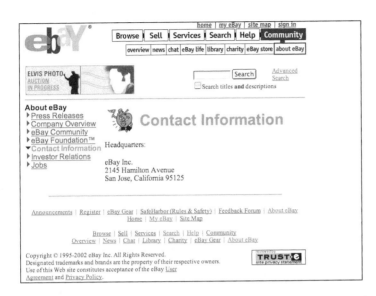

Want to get in touch with someone at eBay? Good luck. The site's contact information page only gives a snail-mail address. This is an unfortunate situation for customers who want assistance via email or telephone. eBay may save money by hiding from its customers, but at what price?

From the customer...

"In my mind it is insane that it is so hard to reach people within eBay. It took me about an hour just to find real eBay phone numbers. I have found that it is impossible to find direct phone numbers and email addresses on the eBay web site.... Isn't it funny that a company that rules the online world forces users to contact them using postal mail?"

Lands' End

HELP THAT'S CONVENIENT FOR YOU   www.landsend.com

Contact Us   Phone   E-mail   Fax   Mailing Address

Here at Lands' End, we've always sold our products directly, so talking with customers is old hat. (And it's a rare Lands' End product that doesn't owe some improvement — or improvements — to customer feedback!) If you have a comment or suggestion, please feel free to contact us in the manner that is most convenient for you.

LANDS' END Live™
Talk to us!

Having problems?
Need questions answered?
Click the Lands' End Live button to talk to us.

Welcome to Lands' End Live™
Talk to us in three easy steps.

1. Choose how you would like to communicate with us
2. Enter your name and phone number
3. Click connect

LANDS' END Live

Talk to us!

⦿ 📞 **Phone**
Choose phone and we will call you. *Requires a second phone line or a direct connection to the internet.*

First name: _____
Last name: _____

Phone Number: _____
U.S. Area Code and Phone Numbers
Ex: 123-456-7890

[Connect]

○ 💬 **Chat**
Choose chat and we can text chat with you. *Does not require a phone.*

Lands' End's "Ask Us" page encourages customers to touch base in whichever way is most convenient: phone, email, fax, or snail mail. Lands' End even offers a live help option that offers immediate support via chat.

4 WAYS TO GET ASSISTANCE

1. **Q & A**

Please select from the options below ▲▼

2. Connect to our Online Customer Service eQ&A Chat. 24 hours a day, seven days a week.

3. Email us a completed customer service form.

4. Call us toll free at 1-800-468-1141

HASSLE-FREE SHOPPING
- Free Returns to Any Gap Store
- Order Status & Tracking
- Credit Card Safeguard & Privacy
- Gap HelpLine: 1.800.GAP.STYLE

1-800-Flowers also offers a range of support options, including chat, email, phone, and FAQs. Gap offers offline solutions (such as returns to any Gap store and a phone help line) as part of their "hassle-free shopping" program.

It's also a good idea to include the hours of operation of call center and chat staffers. 1-800-Flowers mentions online customer service is available 24/7 but fails to give hours for its call center.

GUIDELINE 24

Answer emails quickly and effectively

Your customers took the time to write. Let them know you received their email and make sure you get an answer back to them ASAP (preferably within 24 hours).

Responding quickly and effectively can have a major impact on customer loyalty. According to one survey, 57 percent of customers say the speed of a retailer's response to an email inquiry would affect their decision to make future purchases from them (source: Jupiter Media Metrix).

Ignoring emails or taking days to respond will alienate potential customers. Instead, show you care and be as responsive as possible. Send an auto-response immediately so a customer knows his or her inquiry has reached the proper recipient. Then follow up with a more detailed response to the customer's issue.

Also make sure your copy is written professionally. Poor phrasing or sloppy writing will make your company seem amateurish.

From: gap.com Customer Service
Reply-To: "gap.com Customer Service"
Date: Thursday, May 16, 2002 4:32 PM
To: matt@37signals.com
Subject: Re: GAP-Stores - About Our Products; response-yes

Dear Mr. Ruby,

Thank you for your e-mail. You can use our store locator option
featured on our website. It is located at the right hand corner on our
homepage. If you call the number listed below, you can also obtain this
information by selecting option 3.

If we may be of further assistance, please contact us via e-mail at
custserv@gap.com or by calling 1-800-GAP-STYLE. Our Customer Service
Consultants are here 24 hours a day for your shopping convenience.

Sincerely,

Customer Service Consultant

Original Message Follows:

How can I find the store closest to me?
From-Matthew Ruby ; matt@37signals.com

I sent an email to Gap's customer service department that said, "How can I find the store closest to me?" Within minutes I received an email that acknowledged my question. A few hours later I received this response from Jessica. She gives me specific instructions on how I can find store locations (via the site or by phone) and provides me with Gap's free, 24-hour customer service phone number in case I need more information.

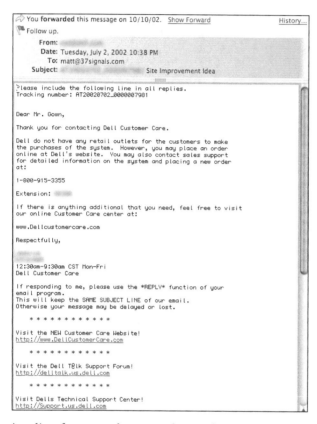

Does Dell have retail outlets? I asked that question to Dell's customer support team and received this bumbling response that states:

"Dell do not have any retail outlets for the customers to make the purchases of the system."

Has Dell hired Tarzan to correspond with customers? If I buy a PC from Dell, will the company be able to provide clear support or will I get more of the same grammatically challenged copy? Although poor grammar may seem like a minor flub, it damages a company's credibility and can cause potential customers to lose faith in a site's support staff.

This email is difficult to understand in other ways, too. The subject line features a long number and generic title that isn't appropriate for the message's content. In the body of the message, the company provides a phone number but doesn't clearly indicate whether that number is exclusively for sales or can handle other customer inquiries, too.

I'm also confused by Jessica's signature, which includes the hours "12:30am–9:30am CST Mon–Fri." Is that her work hours? The hours that Dell Customer Care is open? The hours that phone support is offered? It's difficult to tell. On a brighter note, the company does do a good job of providing links to online support options.

Here are some tips for making support emails helpful:

- Provide a clear, accurate subject line. (Don't title the email with confusing code or internal jargon.)
- Use a functional return address so that customers can reply easily.
- The first paragraph should offer a clear summary of the email's contents.
- Use tracking numbers or some other technique so that customers and support team members can refer to previous exchanges. Often, this is best placed in the email subject line (like this: "Re: Original Subject Line [Case #…]") for tracking purposes.
- Cite the original question or message, because visitors may not remember it otherwise.
- Explain what the reader should do next if the issue remains unresolved.
- If you send the reader to your site, make sure the contents of the landing page logically follow the email you sent.
- Provide the reader with additional support contacts (for instance, call center or online help) and their hours of operation, if appropriate.
- Sign the email so that readers know who at your company sent it.
- Most importantly, answer the question that was asked!

From: landsend@landsend.com
Date: Wednesday, December 4, 2002 8:35 AM
To: scott@37signals.com
Subject: [email report] General Comments
Resent- Scott Upton <scott@37signals.com>
Resent-From: Matt Linderman <matt@37signals.com>
Resent-Date: Wednesday, December 4, 2002 8:35 AM

```
Please include the following line in all replies.
Tracking number:

Dear Scott Upton,

Thank you for your message to Lands' End about our return policy.

Everything Lands' End sells is Guaranteed Period.

There is no time limit on returns.

Typically paying return shipping is the buyer's responsibility.
Under some circumstances we will make other arrangements.

If you place a reorder in connection with the return there is
no shipping charge. To get this free shipping you must place
the reorder in the package with the return or contact us by phone.

If you have other questions about returns or if we may be of
further assistance, please let us know.

Sincerely,


Internet Customer Service
www.landsend.com
1-800-963-4816

>  -----Original Message-----
> From: <scott@37signals.com>
> Sent: 03 Dec 02 11:52
> To: <landsend@landsend.com>
>
>   The following message concerning General Comments was received
> from Scott Upton <scott@37signals.com>.
> ---------------------------------------------------------
>
> I have a few questions about your company's return policy:
>
> 1) What is your return policy?
> 2) How much time do I have in order to return the product after I have
> received it?
> 3) Who pays return shipping if the product doesn't meet my
> expectations?
>
> Thanks.
>
```

This Lands' End email shows a nice human touch. Richard K. makes his point quickly and succinctly and does a good job of addressing each of the three different questions regarding the company's return policy.

The note could provide more information on alternative support options, however. Is there an area of the site that deals with the topic of returns? And what hours are call center operators available?

If you're like me, you have dozens of login names and passwords at different sites. It's difficult to keep all this login information straight.

Site owners shouldn't expect total recall from customers. Help out by offering a hint or email service to remind forgetful visitors of account information.

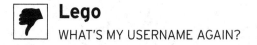

Lego
WHAT'S MY USERNAME AGAIN?

club.lego.com

Lego's site fails to offer assistance to visitors experiencing login difficulties. This means it's tough luck for anyone who can't remember his or her password. The site would be wise to offer a help link that says, "Trouble with login? Forget your password? Click here for help."

Pottery Barn
PASSWORD SAVIOR

www.potterybarn.com

Pottery Barn looks out for customers who have forgotten their password. Click the button and the company will send the right password to the email address associated with the account.

As if...

Why is this good? It's as if I lose the keys to my apartment. I call my superintendent who quickly arrives and unlocks the door. He also gives me a spare key to use in the future.

Yahoo!

GIVE ME A HINT

I submitted an invalid password at Yahoo! The site returns a page with hints on why my login may have failed and a link to recover my ID and/or password.

Apple

THREE STRIKES AND YOU'RE SENT AN EMAIL

It's in the mail.

Thank you. We have sent your Apple ID information to ernest@37signals.com.

When you receive your sign in information, please continue with your shopping

After three failed login attempts, Apple's online store automatically sends my username and password to the account's registered email address. This active assistance is a nifty way to step in before customers get too frustrated. Plus, it shows customers you understand and care about their difficulties.

CHAPTER SUMMARY

Use contextual help to answer questions on the same page they arise. Also offer a clearly marked "Help" area and call it "Help" or something equally obvious. "Help" should be an obvious link from your home page and in the main navigation area on all pages. Carefully organize "Help" so that it's easy for visitors to get to the right piece of information. Self-help options such as community help boards and online training sessions let people find answers on their own. Offer additional support paths such as email, telephone, or live chat. When customers write you, get an answer back to them ASAP (preferably within 24 hours). Also send an auto-response immediately. Help out forgetful visitors by offering a hint or email service to remind them of login information.

Chapter Seven

GET OUT OF THE WAY

Eliminate obstacles to conversion (e.g. unnecessary ads, registration, navigation, etc.)

Guidelines covered in this chapter

26 Don't disable the browser's Back button.

27 Make it fast, not cute.

28 Don't force registration.

29 Don't block content with ads.

30 Eliminate unnecessary navigation during multistep processes.

INTRODUCTION

If you're not part of the solution…

At crisis points, you want to make sure your site is empowering customers in trouble, not compounding the problem. That's why you need to make sure your site doesn't cripple browsers, force registration, use unnecessarily verbose text, or throw ads up at the wrong time.

Sometimes the best way to help visitors is to get out of their way. Efficient contingency design removes anything that isn't essential and provides a streamlined recovery route.

GUIDELINE 26

Don't disable the browser's Back button

The Back button is a powerful escape and navigation tool for web surfers. Just think how often you use it in daily activities while surfing the web.

Unfortunately, many sites don't respect the power of Back. Some order customers to keep moving forward. Others employ code that causes the browser's Back button to cease functioning properly. (For instance, visitors lose any data entered on previous pages or can't actually go back to a previous page.) These disarming tactics disable visitors and can lead to bailouts.

Ticketmaster
BACK ISN'T A BAD REQUEST

www.ticketmaster.com

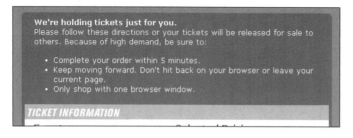

I was attempting to purchase concert tickets when Ticketmaster's server got stuck on the first screen shown here. Normally, I'd click Back and resubmit the form, but Ticketmaster instructs me to "Keep moving forward. Don't hit back on your browser or leave your current page."

The hung server gives me little choice, however. So I ignore the warning and click Back anyway. That's when the second screen appeared detailing my "bad request." Back shouldn't be a "bad request." Ticketmaster's unyielding structure is so frustrating that my only choices are to start over or give up.

eBay
INPUT (T)ERROR

www.ebay.com

This eBay error page tells me to "go back and ensure that all fields are properly filled in." The problem is when I click the browser Back button, *this same page reloads*. I'm trapped in an endless "Input Error" loop! Sounds more like input terror to me.

The lesson: Customers rely on the Back button. In processes like this, make sure they can go back and resubmit form information at the previous page. If they have to start over from scratch, there's a good chance they won't even bother.

# Expedia
BACK = NO PROBLEM

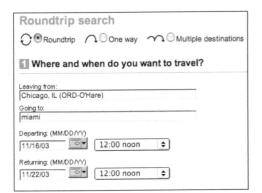

Back is no problem at Expedia. I entered flight information and performed a search. Unfortunately, I didn't like any of the flights that were displayed. I clicked Back and returned to the search page. The information I entered is displayed again, so I can quickly tweak my search criteria and try again. A flawless Back experience like this can help convert customers.

GUIDELINE 27

Make it fast, not cute

Slow-loading pages, large blocks of text, or inappropriate wit can make crisis points even more daunting and difficult to overcome. When visitors are in trouble, get to the point and then get out of the way.

To do this, you may have to review your templates and make sure they are appropriate for all contingencies. A template that makes sense for the rest of your site may seem out of context when problems occur.

Star Wars
EPISODE UGH

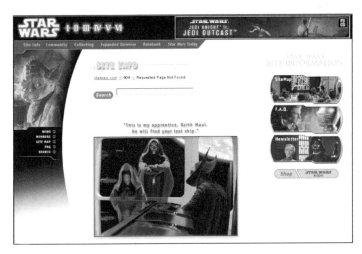

Why does this Star Wars "Page Not Found" screen contain so much irrelevant information? The page contains several large images, an ad banner, and a cutesy message. (That is, "This is my apprentice, Darth Maul. He will help you find your ship.") Meanwhile, the error message—the most important information on the page—is barely noticeable amidst all the visual noise. The site should strip out the extra images and emphasize the error information. (See Guideline 16 in Chapter 5 for help in creating useful "Page Not Found" screens.)

As if...

Why is this bad? It's as if I call 911 and the operator starts telling me a knock-knock joke.

EXPN
TOO CUTE

www.expn.com

OOPS!
Your Team: Marvin Gardens
Your League: The Football League of Canada

Could not continue scan with NOLOCK due to data movement. Severity 12, State 3, Pr
sp_getOrderedTeamData', Line 58

Click the "Back" button on your browser to return to the previous page.

No one wants a long-winded, unfunny error message. Even though EXPN appeals to snowboarders and other extreme sports aficionados, the site makes a mistake by injecting unnecessary text into this error message.

When it comes to error messages, use a tone appropriate to the gravity of the situation. You don't have to be deadly serious but you also shouldn't waste time with jokes. The current text could be edited to read simply: "Your page isn't available right now, but we're working on it. Please check back soon." At least the site does offer a clear headline for the message.

Thrifty
GETTING TO THE POINT

www.thrifty.com

Thrifty's error messages are direct and to the point. The site realizes a crisis point isn't the place to be cute.

Comedy Central
PLAYING IT STRAIGHT

shop.comedycentral.com

Some information in your billing address is either incomplete or needs to be corrected. Please see below:

• Please enter an address title.
• Please enter a city.

Comedy Central goes for laughs most of the time. But not when it comes to error messages. I left a couple of fields blank at the site's store area and the result is this workmanlike, but effective, message.

GUIDELINE 28
Don't force registration

When things fall apart, customers head for "Help." If you want to hold on to these troubled visitors, don't force them to fill out a form to receive assistance. Give them immediate access to the support information that can help them overcome difficulties.

Apple

DON'T MAKE ME SIGN IN FOR HELP

www.apple.com

Here, Apple adds to customer frustration by requiring registration (or login) to get assistance with a faulty product. After hours of frustration, the last thing I wanted to do was spend additional time filling out a registration screen for the company responsible for my problem. Why does the site need additional information that doesn't pertain to the issue at hand?

Registration is one of the most common bailout points for web sites. Don't impose it on customers who are already experiencing difficulties.

As if...

Why is this bad? It's as if I call the phone company to report a problem with my service. To receive assistance, however, I must first sign up for their customer mailing list.

Sun
GETTING TO THE POINT   www.sun.com

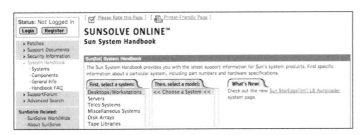

Sun allows visitors to access its support database without logging in. Instead of further frustration, customers get direct access to potential solutions. Meanwhile, Sun saves money because it doesn't need to field additional phone calls, complaints, or help requests.

From the customer...

"I absolutely abhor the practice of demanding registration simply to browse technical articles."

GUIDELINE 29

Don't block content with ads

Critical content shouldn't be obstructed by ads or promotional offerings. This is especially true for error message screens and other crisis points. Ad revenues are important, but your site will lose money if they come at the expense of driving customers away for good.

As the About.com home page finished loading, I started to see something moving above the content. It circled the screen and grew in size until I finally recognized it as an owl promoting the new "Harry Potter" flick. How am I supposed to interact with the site's contents when I'm being attacked by a flying owl?

Abusive advertising like this is not the way to build a loyal following. When visitors see "in-your-face" tactics such as this at a site's home page, they go away and don't come back.

From the customer...

"So you're saying that as a consumer, I have to shut up and take my medicine? That's not gonna happen. [When] people see a highly intrusive ad, they don't say to themselves, 'Hmm, I guess viewing this ad, while keeping me from the task I'm trying to accomplish, is the price I have to pay for this wonderful content.' No, they get cheesed off and either figure out a way around it, or leave altogether."

Yahoo! makes it impossible to sign out of its "Travel" section until this interstitial advertisement is done playing. Ads shouldn't block crucial functionality such as this.

As if...

Why is this bad? It's as if I'm at a travel agency and I want to exit but the agent blocks the door and keeps handing me brochures.

From the customer...

"What these sites don't realize is that these types of ads do much more damage than they can imagine."

"This form of advertising is truly obnoxious ... I can appreciate the difficult economic climate, but I don't think this is an effective way to endear people to click through to the advertising."

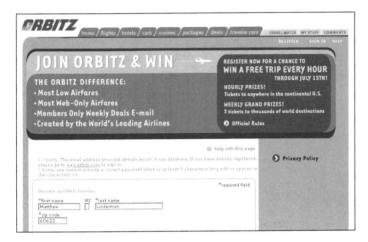

Error pages are a particularly bad place to blitz viewers with unwanted ads and promotional offers. Compare the size of the large ad banner to the tiny error message on this screen at Orbitz. The ad banner is so dominant that visitors may not even notice the more important error information below it.

Needless to say, the error message should take precedence at any crisis point. Orbitz should show customers it is sensitive to their difficulties by omitting advertising from this error screen. It's the right thing to do and the best way to get customers through the form.

From the customer...

"Who would want their ad to appear on an error page? ... All people are going to want to do when they get this sort of error is to find out what went wrong, and what they can do to sort it out."

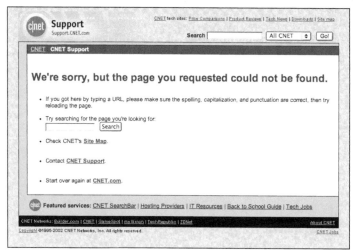

News.com normally features an ad banner at the top of each page, as shown in the first image. The site realizes that ads aren't always appropriate, however. When an error occurs, the site wisely loses its normal template and offers an error page without any ads. (The second screen shows the bannerless "Page Not Found" screen.) This technique is an effective way to show customers your site cares and is doing all it can to help them accomplish their goals.

GUIDELINE 30

Eliminate unnecessary navigation during multi-step processes

During multi-step processes such as checkout or registration, unnecessary navigation options may act as an obstacle to customers. Eliminate extraneous elements so that visitors can complete the task at hand without distraction.

Just make sure you *still offer some way out*. Although you want to help customers complete forms, you don't want them to feel trapped against their will.

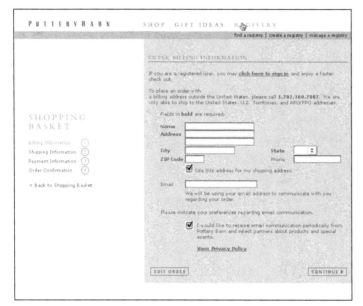

My Pottery Barn cart is stocked, and I've begun to check out. So why, in the midst of the checkout process, is the site's standard navigation bar still at the top of the screen? Instead, the site should offer a simple link out of the checkout process while eliminating the other navigation options. This would prevent an accidental misclick that could derail the entire checkout process.

eBay's site normally displays a navigation bar with 10 options at the top of each page (see screen one). During the sign-up process (screen two), eBay keeps users on track by eliminating the navigation bar and offering just one link (back to home). By eliminating the extra links, eBay keeps customers in the funnel and helps them finish the sign-up process.

CHAPTER SUMMARY

Sometimes the best way to help visitors is to get out of their way. Always make sure the Back button functions normally throughout your site. It is a powerful escape and navigation tool for web surfers. Crisis points aren't good places to be cute, so get to the point and then get out of the way.

Also, check your templates to ensure they are appropriate for all contingencies. A template that makes sense for the rest of your site may seem out of context when problems occur. Don't force frustrated customers to log in or fill out a registration form before receiving assistance. Error message screens and other crisis points shouldn't be obstructed by ads or promotional offerings. Eliminate extraneous navigation elements during multi-step processes such as checkout or registration so that visitors can complete the task at hand without distraction.

Chapter Eight

SEARCH AND RESCUE

Deliver the right results with smart search engine assistance

Guidelines covered in this chapter

31 Offer a clear explanation when no results are found or inexact matches are shown.

32 Anticipate common errors and provide relevant results.

33 Too many results? Offer features that let searchers refine and filter results.

34 No results? Let customers easily expand search criteria.

35 Offer tips on how to improve results.

36 Don't rely on advanced searches.

INTRODUCTION

Too many online searches end in disappointment. Irrelevant results, no results, or an overwhelming number of results impossible to digest are all common-place. When a search fails or frustrates like this, customers are likely to give up on the site as a whole. ("If Search is broken, can Checkout or Shipping be trusted?")

Giving Up

"If users don't find the result with their first query, they are progressively less and less likely to succeed with additional searches. Many users don't even bother: In our study, almost half the users whose first search failed gave up immediately."

—Jakob Nielsen's Alertbox, May 13, 2001: "Search: Visible and Simple"

Many sites focus on best-case search scenarios and ignore imperfect search contingencies. This is a dangerous pattern because even the best search engines are flawed at times. Instead, anticipate problem spots for searchers. When a search goes wrong, offer a plan B that gets visitors to the right product or information.

Can't find an exact match for a visitor's search? Be upfront about it. The fact that no results are found should be the first thing someone sees when a search fails. Clearly state there are no exact matches and offer an explanation if you have one.

If your site offers "close but not quite" alternative results (see Guideline 32), make sure you explain the gap between the search query and the results displayed. Otherwise you may confuse visitors by showing results that are irrelevant to the original search. This can call your entire site's credibility into question.

"Here are the relevant search results for 'caffeine free,'" reads the sentence at the top of this Pepsi search results screen. The problem is there aren't actually any results listed. Are there matches that aren't displaying properly? Or is "caffeine free" nowhere to be found on the site? If it's the latter, the site should clearly state, "No results found for 'caffeine free.'" Then, Pepsi could offer a way to broaden the search (see Guideline 34) or tips on how to improve results (see Guideline 35).

Target
A MOP THAT PLAYS MP3S?

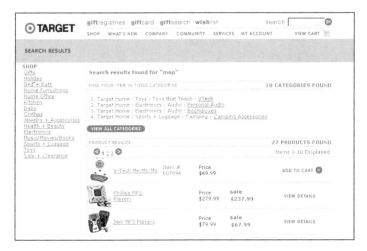

Could it be that Target no longer sells mops? A search for "mop" at Target's site returns results for toys and MP3 players, but nothing bearing any resemblance to a mop. Target is attempting to provide a "smart search" (note how *MP3* and *mop* vary by just one letter), but customers don't know that. To the average Joe, this site looks out of order. Many won't even bother giving it a second chance.

As if...

Why is this bad? It's as if I go to Target and ask customer service where the mops are and they send me to the electronics section.

Although no search engine is 100-percent successful, Target should do more to explain the wide chasm between the search query and the results shown here. A header such as this would at least help minimize the confusion: "No results found for 'mop.' Are any of these results what you were looking for?"

Spun

NO KEYWORD MATCHES

www.spun.com

Spun sells CDs but do they also carry stereo accessories? I searched for "speaker cable," but the site has no links for this term. Thankfully, the site clearly says, "There are no keyword matches for speaker cable." The site could also let customers easily expand searches (see Guideline 34) and provide helpful tips on how to improve results (see Guideline 35).

Crate & Barrel

VOTIVE EXPLANATION

www.crateandbarrel.com

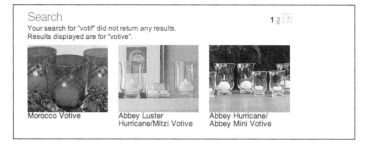

I searched for "votif" at Crate and Barrel's site. No matches were found, but the site wisely directed me to results for "votive." Crate and Barrel also goes out of its way to explain why the results differ from the original term that I searched for. Many sites leave out this important piece of information. Without the note, customers may wonder, "Why did they show me results for 'votive' rather than 'votif?'" The explanation also educates searchers so they won't repeat the same mistake in the future.

A search for "Nike" comes up empty.

Marshall Field's

www.marshallfields.com

Search results found for "nike"

FIND YOUR ITEM IN THESE CATEGORIES...   10 CATEGORIES FOUND

1. Marshall Field's Home : Men : Accessories : Small Leather Goods and Luggage
2. Marshall Field's Home : Women : Jewelry : Fine Jewelry : Gold Jewelry
3. Marshall Field's Home : Home : Tabletop : Silver Giftware : Nambé
4. Marshall Field's Home : Home : Collectibles : Lladró®

VIEW ALL CATEGORIES

PRODUCT RESULTS   14 PRODUCTS FOUND

◀ 1 2 ▶   Items 1-10 Displayed

Cigar Cases		Price $25.00	VIEW DETAILS
14K Gold Polished Hoop Earrings	Item # 05865	Price $200.00	ADD TO BAG
Nambé Tri-Corner Bowl		Price $125.00 - $175.00	VIEW DETAILS
Lladró Graceful Landing	Item # 600353	Price $155.00	ADD TO BAG
Atlantis Nova Wine Set (5-pc.)	Item # 98093	Price $150.00	sale $119.99	ADD TO BAG
Bosca Old Leather Credit Card Case and Wallet		Price $35.00 - $45.00	VIEW DETAILS
Frango® Wedding Favor Mint Coffee Spoons	Item # 11874	Price $20.00	ADD TO BAG
the supernaturals		Price $15.00 - $20.00	VIEW DETAILS
Marketplace Fair Poster	Item # 627369	Price $20.00	sale $14.00	ADD TO BAG

I typed in "Nike" at the site for Marshall Field's, a department store. Instead of sneakers, I got results that had nothing to do with the footwear and athletic-apparel company (for instance, cigar cases, hoop earrings, and a five-piece wine set). The site doesn't provide any explanation for the irrelevant results. It's unlikely I'd want to use Marshall Field's search again.

 **Sears**

www.sears.com

Footwear is currently not available on sears.com. Please try a Sears store near you.

A search for "Nike" at Sears reveals the site doesn't carry footwear online. Thankfully, the site doesn't give me unhelpful results or peddle unrelated products that are merely a poor substitute for the shoes I want. Instead, Sears tells me why I can't find any shoes online and then gives me a link to the Sears store locator so that I can find an offline location to purchase footwear. Even though the site doesn't have the item I need, I'm comforted by the fact that someone at Sears is looking out for customers.

GUIDELINE 32

Anticipate common errors and provide relevant results

A small mistake shouldn't cause the entire search process to break down. Help visitors get to the correct results by anticipating imperfect matches. If it's a mistake you can predict, plan for it.

Your search should be able to map these sorts of common mistakes and provide alternative matches to helpful results:

Errors	Examples
Synonyms	"jacket" and "coat"
Plurals	"computers" and "computer"
Punctuation	"ATM" and "A.T.M."
Case sensitivity	"iPod" and "ipod"
Hyphenations	"Hewlett-Packard" and "Hewlett Packard"
Abbreviations	"Automated Teller Machine" and "A.T.M."
Spelling errors	"sergeant" and "sargeant"
Typos	"candles" and "candels"
English variations	"color" and "colour"

Make sure your site uses search software that plans for these search contingencies. A human touch is also needed, however. Scour your search logs to find out where searches are going bad. Identify trouble spots and intervene to prevent dead-end searches.

IRS

W2 OR W-2?

www.irs.gov

You'd think the IRS would realize that a visitor searching for "W2" is probably hunting for a "W-2" tax form. Not so. Leaving out the dash between the "W" and the "2" returns results that have nothing to do with the form. Aren't taxpayers already disgruntled enough without this sort of lackluster search response? The IRS should check its search query logs to discover common variations such as this one and then map them to the proper results.

Google

BAD SPELLING = NO PROBLEM

www.google.com

Even if you can't spell, Google usually gets you to the results you want. Here, the site spots the misspelled "contingentsy design" and converts it to "contingency design." Built-in spell checkers such as this are a great safety net for searches. Also, note how Google explains the spell-check conversion so that visitors understand what's going on.

Spell check won't catch every invalid search term, however. Names, products, or other terms may be misspelled yet not caught via spell check. Your site's search engine should still be able to redirect wrong terms that are frequently entered, even if basic spell checking doesn't reveal the problem.

How Do I Choose a Search Engine for My Site?

There are many factors to consider when choosing a search for your site (for instance, price, platform, and ease of installation). Research the options online at Search Tools (http://www.searchtools.com), a site that offers information, news, and advice about web site searching technology. The site explains how to choose, implement, and maintain search tools and also offers links to books, reports, and articles on the topic.

I search for information on ADSX, a stock that, unbeknownst to me, recently changed symbols to ADSXE.

 **MarketWatch**

www.marketwatch.com

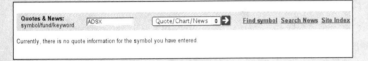

The site informs me "there is no quote information" for ADSX. This strikes me as rather odd because the symbol worked fine last time I checked. Therefore, I'm left to wonder, "What happened?" Confused, I decide to check the stock elsewhere.

Yahoo! Finance

Symbol ADSX	Ticker symbol has changed to: ADSXE.

The site tells me the ticker symbol has changed to ADSXE and links that symbol to the correct stock listing. Yahoo! realizes that investors often track many stocks and won't always be up to speed on recent ticker changes. The message is brief and effective.

Amazon
YOU KNOW WHAT I MEAN   www.amazon.com

> We found no matches for **neal diamond**. Below are results for **neil diamond**.

Online music retailers should expect some customers to make the mistake of searching for "Neal Diamond." (He actually spells his first name with an *i*.) Search for "Neal Diamond" at Amazon and the site is smart enough to return the correct set of results, preceded by this message: "We found no matches for neal diamond. Below are results for neil diamond." This is a great way to impress customers and increase sales.

From the customer...

"When I shop online, I am generally looking for a specific item. If I know a particular e-commerce site permits me to find what I am looking for quickly and easily, I go there first. Also, if the company has clearly spent effort to perfect a fast and effective search process, I automatically assume that everything else about them (billing, shipping, returns, etc) will be 'dialed in.'"

```
488941 britney spears
 40134 brittany spears
 36315 brittney spears
 24342 britany spears
  7331 britny spears
  6633 briteny spears
  2696 britteny spears
  1807 briney spears
  1635 brittny spears
  1479 brintey spears
  1479 britanny spears
  1338 britiny spears
  1211 britnet spears
  1096 britiney spears
   991 britaney spears
   991 britnay spears
   811 brithney spears
   811 brtiney spears
   664 birtney spears
   664 brintney spears
   664 briteney spears
   601 bitney spears
   601 brinty spears
   544 brittaney spears
   544 brittnay spears
   364 britey spears
   364 brittiny spears
```

Previous search queries can help you identify common errors. Google, for example, studies search logs to identify problem spots and then guides visitors around potential pitfalls. This means searchers get the desired results with minimal friction.

The data in the first image shows misspellings detected by Google's spelling correction system for the query "Britney Spears." (The number to the left of each entry is the number of different searchers who spelled her name that way within a 3-month period.) In that time, more than 40,000 visitors mistakenly entered "Brittany Spears" as a search query.

To help out pop fans, the site offers this link, with the correct spelling, on the resulting page: "Did you mean: Britney Spears?" (image two). Even if a visitor misspells Britney's name, the correct results are still just a click away.

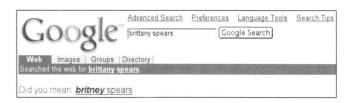

From the customer...

"Google rocks. I swear it can read my mind, despite my spelling errors, lack of articulation, and so on. I love Google."

Analyzing Search Logs

Use your logs to identify keywords that are commonly entered yet not found at your site. Then intervene and map these searches to the right results. Also, note top searches and highlight these "most popular" items when delivering results (see Guideline 33).

You can also use this information to examine the effectiveness of information architecture and navigation. For example: Are visitors frequently searching for terms such as "jobs" and "careers?" If so, check to see whether the relevant link is confusingly titled (for instance, "Be One Of Us") or available only through a hard-to-find pulldown menu.

Bluelight

www.bluelight.com

Bluelight notifies me it is "having trouble locating a match" for my search term—even though the site does carry Farberware products. Oblivious to the misspelling, I take my business elsewhere.

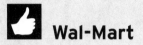

Wal-Mart

www.walmart.com

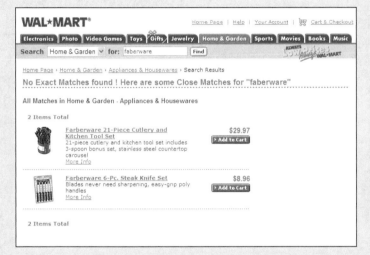

Despite the misspelling, Wal-Mart presents me with a list of items produced by Farberware. Included in the list is the kitchen organizer that I was looking for.

After all, would an offline Wal-Mart store turn me away if I mispronounced a product's name to a sales clerk? Of course not. Wal-Mart understands this and makes sure to account for common misspellings, the online equivalent of poor pronunciation.

GUIDELINE 33

Too many results? Offer features that let searchers refine and filter results.

Searching for items at many sites is as painstaking as mining for gold; you have to sift through a lot of worthless dirt to find the occasional nugget of value.

Although providing too many results may seem like a good problem to have ("Hey, it's better than nothing, right?"), the truth is most customers aren't willing to invest the time or energy required to sort through an avalanche of results. This is especially true when the top results bear little or no resemblance to the desired item.

Best Buy

I JUST WANTED A DVD PLAYER!

Burying the right results among dozens of wrong items makes shopping a real chore. Here, a search for "DVD player" at Best Buy returns an avalanche of results, including lens cleaner, video cable, audio cable, and, somewhere in the middle of it all, a few actual DVD players. To make matters worse, Best Buy offers no way to filter or sort the results. With all this noise, it's unlikely that a customer will find the right item. A negative search experience like this can drive a customer away permanently.

As if...

Why is this bad? It's as if I go to a clothing store and ask a clerk where the long sleeve t-shirts are kept. He points to a pile of clothes lying on the floor and says, "I bet there's one somewhere in the pile. You can go ahead and check."

Although options are a good thing, remember that too many results can be overwhelming. Visitors turn to search to quickly find desired products, information, or other items. A search shouldn't feel like an expedition. Empower customers by providing tools that enable them to easily sort through large batches of results.

Organizing search results

These features can help customers "find the gold" amid a ton of search results:

1. List item categories.
2. Place most popular items first.
3. Provide sort functionality.
4. Offer filtering tools to narrow results.
5. Point visitors to related items.

Let's take a closer look at how sites use each of these techniques to help searchers.

List item categories

Offer results by category (in addition to individual items) so that searchers can drill down to relevant information.

L.L. Bean

GIVE ME THE BOOT   www.llbean.com

Search results for: "boots"

Your search returned **301** result(s), sorted I

Men's	(68 results)
Women's	(62 results)
Kids'	(27 results)
Outdoor Gear & Apparel	(134 results)
Home & Outdoor Living	(6 results)
On Sale!	(3 results)

Now showing results **1-20**

MEN'S
Accessories & Underwear: <u>Socks</u>

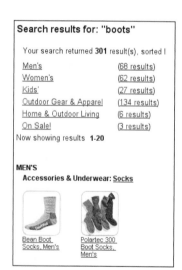

Bean Boot Socks, Men's   Polartec 300 Boot Socks, Men's

I searched for "boots" at L.L. Bean. The results page starts with a list of categories allowing me to go directly to the results I want (in the Men's section) while excluding irrelevant results. This way I don't have to comb through all the women's and kid's boots that also matched my search.

Place most popular items first

Customers rarely make it past the first page or two of search results. That's why the "above-the-fold" results that customers see first are crucial. Putting the most popular (or most relevant) items first increases the odds that you'll return the right information.

Amazon
WHICH CASH?

www.amazon.com

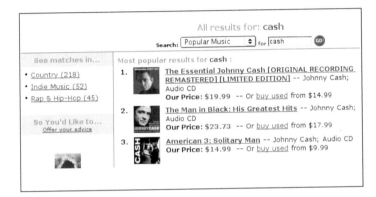

I went to Amazon's music section and searched for "Cash"—but am I looking for country legend Johnny Cash, hip-hop act Cash Money, or another "Cash" artist? Amazon uses existing data to figure out which "Cash" results are most popular and offers me these items first.

Provide sort functionality

A large list of results is less intimidating when visitors can determine the order.

Sears

SORT OPTIONS

www.sears.com

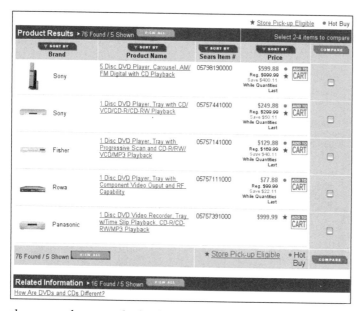

There are 76 results found for "dvd player" at Sears. Despite the large number of items, Sears makes sure the searcher stays in control by offering easy-to-use sort functionality. If you're broke, you can sort by price. Sony fanatic? Then sort by brand. Either way, Sears is smart enough to let shoppers decide which item attributes are most important. The site's interface should graphically indicate which column is the sort column and whether the sort is ascending or descending, however.

Citysearch

HAVE IT YOUR WAY

www.citysearch.com

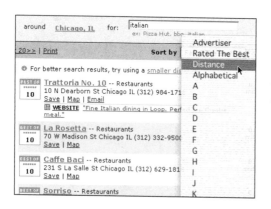

Hundreds of restaurants match my search criteria at Citysearch. Thankfully, the site offers a pull-down menu that enables me to sort the results by popularity, distance, or alphabetical order.

Offer filtering tools to narrow results

Whereas sort merely rearranges results, filter actually eliminates results that are deemed irrelevant. This enables customers to separate the wheat from the chaff.

Yahoo!
NARROW MY SEARCH

www.yahoo.com

Visitors appreciate the ability to winnow results by searching within a found set. Here, Yahoo! Personals enables me to narrow a large number of results down to a manageable number. The site gives me the power to choose my most important criteria and then filters the results accordingly.

HotJobs
REFINE RESULTS

www.hotjobs.com

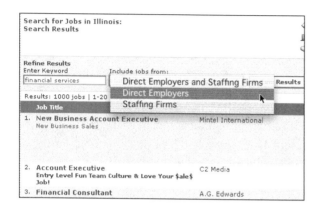

A thousand job listings are too many to sort through. That's why HotJobs enables me to refine these results by keyword and type of listing (from a direct employer, staffing firm, or both). This reduces the listings to a dozen or so, a number I can handle.

eBay
GET MORE SPECIFIC

www.ebay.com

A general search at eBay for a jacket or watch will return a flood of results. That's why the site offers filtering tools alongside search results. You can filter jackets by style, size, color, material, or price. Watches can be narrowed via brand, gender, style, features, age, or price. This allows customers to get to the right product without having to wade through unwanted items.

Point visitors to related items

Recommendation information can be an effective way to guide customers to desired content. Just make sure your related items are suggested in a nonintrusive way.

Qwest

SUGGEST RELATED DOCUMENTS   www.qwest.com

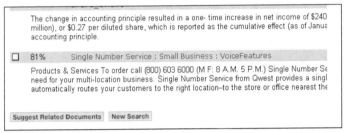

A search at Qwest returns many pages of results to sort through. I welcomed the Suggest Related Documents button at the bottom of the page as a tool to narrow my search.

I checked the results that looked like they were headed in the right direction (each search result starts with a check box), clicked the button, and quickly refined the results.

CDNow

IF YOU LIKE THIS...   www.cdnow.com

At CDNow, I searched for "No Doubt." The site returned results for the band and also offered me links to artists in related genres. This means I can find similar artists without starting the search process over again. When you combine all of these techniques, large result sets become less daunting.

HEAD TO HEAD
Too Many Results

I search a sporting goods web site for "basketball shoes." A large number of responses match my search query.

 Foot Locker

www.footlocker.com

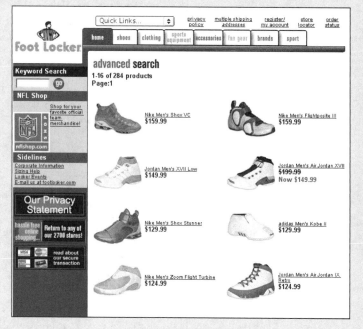

Footlocker displays shoes that match my search query but doesn't provide a way to filter the results. My only options are to choose one of the products shown or click through to the next screen to see more results. But would any customer really be willing to click through 17 pages to see all these shoes? It's doubtful. Foot Locker should offer tools to eliminate unwanted items.

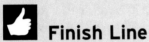 **Finish Line**

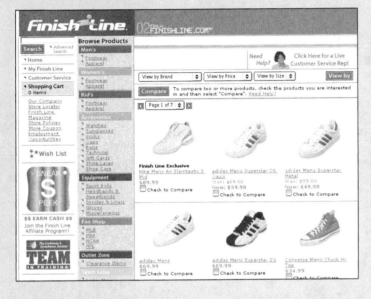

Finish Line gives me the option to filter the results by brand, price, or size. I can also compare various items, jump directly to any of the results pages, or ask a live customer service representative for help. This is a results page that puts the shopper in the driver's seat.

Amazon
LETTING THE CUSTOMER DECIDE

www.amazon.com

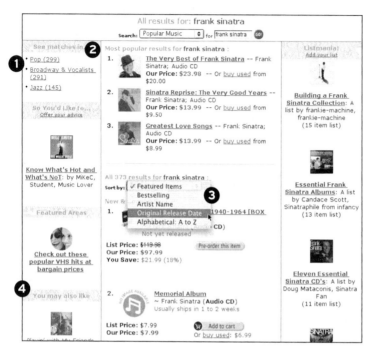

A search for "Frank Sinatra" at Amazon's music area yields 373 results. Instead of just throwing up a list of Sinatra items in seemingly random order, Amazon guides me through the maze of results with useful navigation options:

1. Categories that the results fall under (for instance, Pop or Jazz)

2. Results that start with the most popular items

3. The ability to sort by various criteria (for instance, best-selling, release date, alphabetic)

4. Other related items ("You may also like" features Amazon recommendations, and "Listmania" provides suggestions from other customers.)

GUIDELINE 34

No results? Let customers easily expand search criteria.

"No results" pages shouldn't be dead ends. When no results are found, return a screen that explains the lack of results (see Guideline 31) and offers a search feature that lets people easily modify the failed query. This search box should be populated with the original query so that visitors can quickly tweak the text if necessary.

Also, nudge visitors in the right direction when a search fails. Allow them to expand queries via a quick link or check box. If visitors search for a business within 1 mile of their home, you might ask whether they'd like to "Expand search to include businesses within 5 miles of your home." If they search for a term in the titles of product listings, you could ask whether they want to "Search titles and descriptions" instead.

Marriott

NO QUICK FIX

www.marriott.com

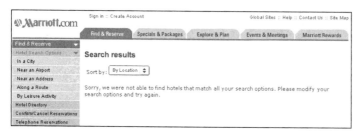

Marriott's site is unable to find a hotel for the location and dates that I entered. The site instructs me to modify my search options and try again. Yet this page doesn't enable me to modify my search criteria. In fact, it doesn't even contain a search box at all. Marriott should display the search location and dates I entered and offer an easy way to alter them from this screen. Also, the "sort by" pull-down should be removed because there aren't any results to sort.

eBay

TRY THESE SEARCH ALTERNATIVES

www.ebay.com

eBay lets me expand my search with just one click. The check box above the Search button expands my search to cover titles and descriptions (the basic search only checks titles). Also, the site populates the search box with the original query (that is, "mens velour suit"), so I can tweak the term without having to retype the whole phrase.

Quick expansion of search parameters from a results page increases the odds visitors will find the desired information. If you fail to offer this functionality, customers will either give up or be forced to start over from scratch.

Yahoo!

NEED MORE RESULTS?

www.yahoo.com

Your search found no results. Please modify your search.

Need more results?

Broaden your search criteria by clicking one of the links below:

- Wider age range: <u>18 - 41</u> | <u>18 - 43</u> | <u>18 - 45</u>
- Larger geographic area: <u>5 mi.</u> | <u>10 mi.</u> | <u>15 mi.</u> | <u>25 mi.</u>
- Photos option: <u>Show ads both with and without photos</u>

Try not to limit your search criteria. Try choosing the "No Preference" or "Any" options.

Because my original search efforts yielded meager results, Yahoo! Personals enables me to broaden my search with just one click. It's a great idea to let customers quickly increase search results like this. It keeps visitors moving forward rather than backward.

As if...

Why is this good? It's as if I ask a hotel concierge if there is a good Italian restaurant on the same block as the hotel. She reports that although there is no restaurant like that on this particular street, there is a great Italian place that's just a few blocks away.

News

EXPAND YOUR SEARCH

www.news.com

Didn't find what you were looking for?

Expand Your Search: ⦿ News.com ◯ CNET
◯ Business Publications ◯ General News ◯ The Entire Web

contingency design [Search]

News.com lets me quickly expand my search to all CNET sites, a wider range of business publications, or even the entire web.

Using your site's search engine may seem like an easy task to you, but it can be a confusing endeavor for outsiders. How can you help? Explain how your site's search works, give examples, and offer helpful tips for obtaining better or more results. This information is especially valuable after a failed search.

Reebok

NO TIPS

www.reebok.com

Reebok's unhelpful search results page doesn't offer any suggestions for improvement. The site should be more proactive and offer tips on how to improve my search.

Amazon

SEARCH EXAMPLES

www.amazon.com

We were unable to find exact matches for your search:

newscroppers

Would you like to search again?

Enter Keywords: [   ] [Search]

Examples:

- Entering **"miles davis"** finds items by and about Miles Davis.
- Entering **"miles blue"** finds items related to Miles Davis's *Kind of Blue* album.
- Entering **"news"** finds items with "news" as a keyword (e.g. the novel *The Shipping News*, CDs by Huey Lewis and the News, the VHS version of *The Bad News Bears*)

Sign up to be e-mailed when new releases for "newscroppers" arrive.

[Continue]

Is there a specific product you'd like us to sell?
Tell us about it.

Amazon reaches out to newbies by displaying examples of how the search engine works. They also offer an email feature for "coming soon" items and to solicit requests for specific products.

AllRecipes

FOR BETTER RESULTS...

www.allrecipes.com

Quick Search results...

Looking for: |brown sugar ⊙
163 results found! Showing **1-25**

Your search exceeds 100 results. That's a lot ...
For better results, try typing in
more specific **words** or **ingredients**.

HINT: Try the following to improve your search results:
- Check your spelling.
- Type in a less specific search word or phrase.
- Read our **search tips**

Allrecipes gives me results for "brown sugar," yet also notes the huge number of results. The site tells me to be more specific and also offers a link to search tips on another page. This increases the odds that I'll get the recipe I need.

From the customer...

"I love allrecipes.com. Not only do they allow you to search by ingredients, or by multiple ingredients, they also allow you to search excluding certain ingredients if you want. Now that's cooking with what's in the kitchen!"

GUIDELINE 36

Don't rely on advanced searches

Complex searches are intimidating to most visitors. That's probably why the vast majority of people never use them. Although an advanced search can be a helpful option for expert users who know the intricacies of your search system, don't rely on it exclusively. Use a simple search as the default option for visitors. If an advanced search is truly helpful, provide it as a supplemental option.

Musician's Friend

TOO COMPLEX

www.musiciansfriend.com

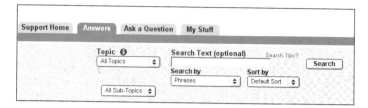

Musician's Friend does a smart thing by offering a search engine that is exclusive to its Help section. Unfortunately, the search interface is much too confusing. The site is trying to empower visitors, but this complex screen provides too many options for most people. The site would be better off offering a plain Jane search rather than this intimidating version.

Palm

PULL-DOWN OVERLOAD

www.palm.com

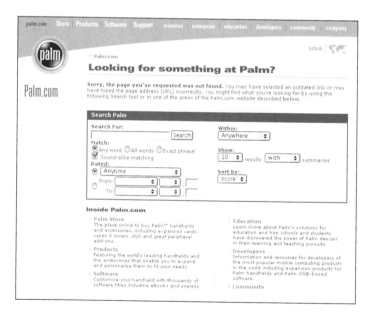

Palm's efforts to provide a search on the site's "Page Not Found" screen is commendable, but the plethora of options will confuse many customers. At a crisis point such as this, it's wiser to stick with a simple search that's easy for everyone to understand.

Chicago Tribune

BASIC FIRST, THEN ADVANCED
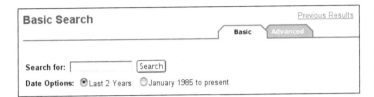

Sites should concentrate on creating bulletproof simple searches before focusing on seldom-used advanced searches.

The Chicago Tribune offers an advanced search for expert visitors but realizes the complexity may be intimidating for others. This tabbed solution is a good compromise. The basic search is offered first with the advanced version just a click away.

CHAPTER SUMMARY

Help frustrated searchers by anticipating problem spots and planning for imperfect search contingencies. Make sure you don't offer inaccurate search results that may erode your site's credibility. Accept common typos, synonyms, and other predictable errors. Study previous search queries to identify problem spots. Most customers aren't willing to invest the time or energy required to sort through an avalanche of results, so offer features that narrow results. If a customer's search yields few or no results, provide an easy way to expand the set of results. Explain how your site's search works, give examples, and offer helpful tips for obtaining better or more results. Complex searches are intimidating to most visitors, so use a simple search as the default option.

Chapter Nine

OUT OF STOCKS AND UNAVAILABLE ITEMS

Make sure unavailable items don't become dead ends

Guidelines covered in this chapter

37 Be upfront about item unavailability.

38 If a product will be available at a later date, explain when, provide product details, and take advance orders.

39 Offer email notification.

40 Show similar items that are available.

INTRODUCTION

Sometimes a product, piece of information, or other item at your site will be unavailable. That's life. These sorts of out of stocks don't have to mean online disaster, however. In fact, they represent a great opportunity to show off quality customer service.

A laissez-faire attitude toward out of stocks leaves customers disappointed. Instead, explain the situation clearly and prevent unwelcome surprises. Let customers pre-order unreleased products or backorder out-of-stock items. Offer to notify them when a product returns to stock. Show alternative items that may work instead.

Unavailable Items

The guidelines in this chapter don't just apply to e-commerce sites. The techniques used for out-of-stock products also can help visitors frustrated by a missing press release, PDF, link, tracking number, and so forth.

Tell customers immediately when an item is unavailable. You'll add insult to injury if you force them to click through several screens before delivering the bad news. Customers appreciate frank, forthright messaging when it comes to critical information such as item availability.

Search results screens need to indicate items that are not actually available. Also, product detail pages should clearly state "Out of Stock" (or something similar) in bold, red text at the top of the page. It's likely to be the most important information on the page for visitors; make it the first thing they notice.

And don't wait until checkout to tell customers something is unavailable. They'll wonder why you didn't inform them sooner.

Baby Ultimate
DON'T TEASE LIKE THAT

Search for: | Jungle Tree Mobile Baby | [Search]

■ = words found   ■ = words found together   ■ = all words found

Jungle Tree Mobile Baby

Baby Mobile. Fabulous designer musical mobile for baby's room features soft, stuffed jungle animals in bright primary colors: zebra, hippo, monkey and lion, as well as a huge ...

Baby Ultimate

Children's Clothing Boutique ~ Preemie to 14   www.babyultimate.com

customer phone
877-724-4537
9:00 - 5:00 Pacific

Jungle Tree Mobile Baby

Baby Mobile. Fabulous designer musical mobile for baby's room features soft, stuffed jungle animals in bright primary colors: zebra, hippo, monkey and lion, as well as a huge jungle tree covering the mobile arm with a sitting monkey atop. The five animals become toy companions after baby outgrows the mobile. Wind up music box plays "Brahms' Lullaby." Includes color coordinated designer arm which can be attached to crib or wall. This whimsical mobile will take the center stage of any nursery! Baby Mobile.

[Add to Wish List]

13179 **$49.95**
SORRY, OUT OF STOCK: [‡]

I was looking for the hard-to-find "Jungle Tree Mobile" around the web but couldn't find it anywhere. Finally, I found the mobile at Baby Ultimate's site. You can imagine my excitement. I clicked through to the product detail page and read the description and the price. It wasn't until I got to the bottom of the screen that I saw this unfortunate message: "Sorry, out of stock." The search results screen should have told me the item was unavailable. And although the product detail page did offer this information, it should be featured prominently at the top of the screen rather than the bottom.

Amazon and Tower Records

STOCK NOTIFICATION   www.amazon.com and www.towerrecords.com

The search results page at Amazon, the first image, clearly shows which books are available and which ones are out of print. This is helpful because it means I don't have to click deeper to discover which books I can actually buy. As an added bonus, Amazon also provides links to used copies of the out-of-print books.

Tower Records, the second image, also does a good job of explaining various stock contingencies. The site specifies which items are in stock, low stock, not yet available, or available via special order. These terms are all linked to their respective definitions (delivered via pop-up windows).

Lands' End
INVENTORY ALERT

www.landsend.com

Inventory Alert

Backordered

Women's Regular Faille Hi-cut Bottom
Size: 14, Item # 69055AK3

We're sorry, this item is not currently in stock. You may still order this backordered item and it will be delivered as soon as we get new stock into our warehouse.

`backorder this item`

You will not be billed until the item is shipped.

Select an alternate item
These similar styles are available.

Women's
Regular Hi-neck
Colorblock
Slender Swimsuit

Women's Long
Hi-neck
Colorblock
Slender Swimsuit

Women's
Regular D-cup
Hi-neck
Colorblock
Slender Swimsuit

Women's Long
D-cup Hi-neck
Colorblock
Slender Swimsuit

I select an unavailable product at Lands' End and the screen immediately notifies me that the item is not currently in stock. The site enables me to backorder the item and suggests alternative items that are similar. Lands' End could probably use a more understandable term than "Inventory Alert," however. "Out of Stock" or "Unavailable Right Now" would work better.

If an item is unavailable, it's important to have a backup plan for customers.

First of all, provide any item details you do have. Visitors still want to know about a product even if they can't obtain it immediately. What's the price? If it's a book, how many pages is it? If it's a sweater, what colors does it come in? If it's a movie, who stars in it?

Also, allow customers to advance order (or backorder) the unavailable item whenever possible. Accept pre-orders for a soon-to-be-released CD. Take backorders for a toy that is out of stock. Many customers will appreciate the opportunity to place an order now instead of being forced to return to the site at a later date.

You'll have to clearly explain the details, however. As early in the process as possible, explain that the item cannot be delivered immediately. Then, explain when it will be available and the ordering options available. You'll probably want to include a caveat, too, because pre-release product details are often subject to change and products that are announced sometimes never ship (or ship at a date much later than originally scheduled). If an item or the ship date changes, send customers an email asking whether they still want to complete the purchase despite the change.

Bookpool
WHEN WILL I GET IT?

www.bookpool.com

Bookpool tells me this book is not in stock yet still allows me to add it to my shopping cart. But why doesn't this screen tell me when it will be delivered? I had to search through the site's Help section to find out that "1 to 3 weeks are required to bring a backordered title into stock." I shouldn't have to hunt for this sort of delivery information. It should be clearly stated on the product details page.

CDNow
EXPECTED RELEASE DATE

www.cdnow.com

What do you do when a visitor selects a product that hasn't been released yet? In this case, CDNow (now part of Amazon) lists the album's expected release date and lets customers order it anyway (or add it to a wish list). If you can't deliver a product immediately, make sure that customers are aware of the delay.

I search for a book that is not yet available.

 ## Barnes & Noble

www.bn.com

Pause and Effect
Mark S Stephen Meadows

Format: Paperback, 320pp.
ISBN: 0735711712
Publisher: New Riders Publishing
Pub. Date: November 2002

This item is not yet available.
Check back at a later date.

Barnes & Noble tells me the item isn't available and recommends I check back later. Several questions linger, however:

- Why can't the site notify me when the book is available?
- Is there any other information, such as price, available?
- And why doesn't Barnes & Noble allow me to pre-order the book?

The site does list a publication date but it's not very specific. (That is, when in November will the book be published?) Overall, the dearth of information leaves me frustrated and unlikely to return.

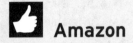 **Amazon**

Pause & Effect: The Art of Interactive Narrative
by Mark Stephen Meadows

List Price: $45.00
Our Price: $31.50
You Save: $13.50 (30%)

This item will be published on August 12, 2002. You may order it now and we will ship it to you when it arrives.
Edition: Paperback

30% off

see larger photo

▸ **See more product details**

READY TO BUY?
Pre-order this item today
or
Sign in to turn on 1-Click ordering.

Add to Wish List
- or -
Add to Wedding Registry
Don't have one?
We'll set one up for you.

Amazon takes a more active approach toward early-bird customers. Although the book is unavailable, Amazon tells me the date the book will be published and the price. The site also lets me pre-order the book and have it shipped when it arrives. Or I can add it to my wish list, an easy way to save this title for future reference. (Email notification, see Guideline 39, would also be nice.) The helpful text explains how and when the order will be completed. This type of customer-centric response is why shoppers trust Amazon.

Don't expect customers to return to your site on a regular basis to check on an item's status. "Check back at a later date" isn't nearly as effective as "Let us tell you when it arrives." Offer to notify customers by email when an out-of-stock product becomes available. Otherwise, they may never come back.

When a customer does submit an email address for notification, immediately send an email to confirm the request. This way the customer knows the request went through and has a copy of it. When the product does become available, send a notice and make sure it includes a direct link to the correct URL.

This is *not* an invitation to serve up unsolicited spam. Unless customers request additional information, don't add them to any other mailing lists.

UPS
CAN'T YOU GET BACK TO ME?

www.ups.com

Tracking Number Response

Unable to track shipment "1Z 1A7 15V 03 3471 265 0 ".

We could not find information for this tracking number. Make sure the tracking number is correct and try again.

Message received:

TRACKING NUMBER NOT FOUND IN UPS DATABASE. PLEASE TRY LATER. KAIPAMG3.(1044)

I checked a valid tracking number at the UPS site, but UPS tells me it can't find the number in its database. To make matters worse, the site puts the burden on me to try back later. The number did appear a few hours later, but only after I wasted time checking back several times. A friendlier site would take my email address and notify me when the number is found.

KRS200T
Skater design Tee

Navy Blue on White.

OUT LARGE $10.00

CLICK HERE
TO BE NOTIFIED
WHEN THIS ITEM
IS RESTOCKED

The Kill Rock Stars record label shows how to make the best of a negative stock situation. The site makes it clear, at a glance, that the t-shirt I want is out of stock. Then the site accepts my email address so I can be notified when the shirt becomes available. The site even goes out of its way to tell me that my email address will not be used for any other purposes. Overall, this interaction makes me feel cared for as a customer.

TELL ME WHEN THIS ITEM IS IN STOCK!

Kill Rock Stars

KRS200T
Skater design Tee LARGE

Enter your email address below and we'll email you when it is available. Hotmail and AOL users - don't forget the ".com" at the end of your address!

> GO!

When you click "GO" you will be returned to the page you came from. Your email address will only be used to notify you of the stock status of this item, and will be deleted as soon as we do. To subscribe to the general Kill Rock Stars mailing list, please visit the main page of the KRS site

---

As if...

Why is this good? It's as if a helpful store clerk takes my number and offers to give me a call when the item I want is back in stock.

Action Labs	Avena Sativa, 750 mg, 50 Tabs.	$14.99	$12.45	N/A	Out Of Stock Please notify me when available
Imperial Elixir Ginseng	Chinese Red Ginseng, 500 mg, 50 Caps.	$10.49	$9.69	1	ADD TO CART
Imperial Elixir Ginseng	Chinese Red Panax Ginseng Extractum, 10x10 c.c.	$5.95	$5.28	1	ADD TO CART
Nature's Herbs	Damiana, 100 Caps.	$8.49	$7.05	N/A	Out Of Stock Please notify me when available
Natrol	DHEA, 10 mg, 30 Tabs.	$4.50	$3.85	1	ADD TO CART
Schiff	DHEA, 25 mg, 30 Tabs.	$5.79	$4.38	N/A	Out Of Stock Please notify me when available
Schiff	DHEA, 25 mg, 60 Tabs.	$7.29	$5.46	1	ADD TO CART
Natrol	DHEA, 5 mg, 30 Tabs.	$3.50	$2.97	1	ADD TO CART

http://www.mothernature.com/...ificatio...

Thank you for your request

To be notified when product
Damiana, 100 Caps.
returns to stock, please type your email address in
the box below:

We will watch this product up to 60 days and notify
you via email when it is available. If after 60 days
the item is still not in available, we will assist you
in finding a substitute product.
Date: **14-Oct-2002**

Any questions please call Customer Care at
1-800-439-5506

Submit Request   Cancel

Mother Nature's search results page clearly notes which items can be added to my cart and which ones are out of stock. Thankfully, the out of stocks come with a link that says, "Please notify me when available." The link takes me to a page that tells me that Mother Nature will watch this product and notify me when the item returns to stock. If the item is still unavailable after 60 days, the company will help me find a substitute. The message ends with a support number as well.

Overall, it's a strong presentation but it could be slightly better. If an adequate substitute exists, why make customers wait 60 days to learn about it? Also, there's no real need for the Cancel button here (see Guideline 14, Chapter 4).

GUIDELINE 40

Show similar items that are available

If you can't give customers exactly what they want, try to offer an adequate substitute. If black isn't available, maybe blue will fit the bill. Similar items that are in stock can rescue customers from a negative experience.

Accordion
$20.99
301135
Out-Of-Stock

Here is a genuine, working accordion that kids will love. While small enough (7" x 7" x 4" closed) to be manageable by small hands, the sounds it produces are surprisingly robust. The bellows are constructed of a rubberized fabric, and they are attached to well-constructed molded sidepieces. Seven melody keys on one side provide for fourteen melodic notes (two notes per reed). On the opposite panel reside bass keys, chord keys and an air valve key for easy bellows expansion. A snap-strap closure secures the unit when idle. While technically a toy, our Accordion delivers first-rate sound and is capable of producing real music. It's a must-have instrument for children who are musically curious. Includes instructions. For age 7 through adult.

Quantity 1   Add to Cart   View Cart

This toy accordion at Terrific Toy is out of stock. But is there another accordion available? How about a different toy musical instrument that might suffice? Terrific Toy could increase sales and customer satisfaction by presenting alternatives to out-of-stock items.

Also, the page offers an unexplained "Add to Cart" button even though the item is unavailable. This button conflicts with the out-of-stock message and is likely to confuse customers.

Gap and L.L. Bean

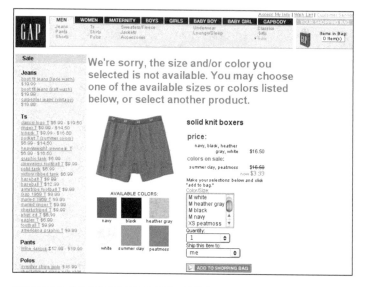

In the first example, Gap tells me that the specific item I selected isn't available. The site then lets me choose from a list of size/color combinations that are available. Note how the site uses a larger font size, bold text, and color variation (red text) to highlight the key message at the top of the screen.

Although L.L. Bean (the second example) doesn't have the color shirt I want, the site offers a list of in-stock alternatives. I can select a different color and then continue on my way.

There's still room for improvement, however. These sites could save shoppers a step by eliminating or flagging unavailable size/color combinations. If I can't take any action (buy, backorder, or get email notification) on a medium, blue item, don't let me select it in the first place.

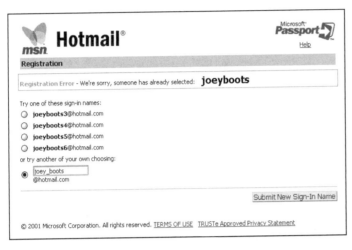

With so many sign-in names already taken, it's difficult to select a unique email address at Hotmail. The site wisely prevents fruitless attempts to pick one by presenting available alternatives that are close to the original choice. In this case, "joeyboots" is unavailable, but the site offers "joeyboots3" and other near matches. Smart suggestions such as these prevent repeat errors and minimize customer frustration.

As if...

Why is this good? It's as if I'm at a fast-food restaurant's drive-through window and order a fried chicken sandwich. The salesperson informs me that although they're out of fried chicken, grilled and barbecue chicken sandwiches are still available.

I try to select a domain name, www.techtips.com, that is already registered.

Domain Bank

www.domainbank.com

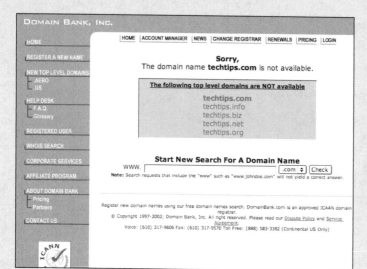

Domain Bank tells me that the domain techtips.com is not available. Then, the site lists other "techtips" domain names that are also unavailable. Unfortunately, Domain Bank doesn't guide me toward any domain names that are available.

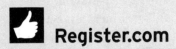 **Register.com**

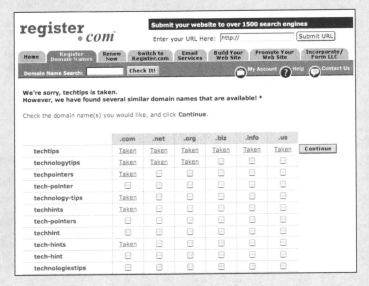

Register.com shows a more proactive approach to the same situation. The site tells me, "We're sorry, techtips is taken. However, we have found several similar domain names that are available." The site then presents a chart of similar domain names and notes which ones are taken and which are still available. Instead of a flat rejection, I have dozens of similar names to choose from.

Why offer up only a closed door if you can present visitors with other open ones?

CHAPTER SUMMARY

Out-of-stock and unavailable items don't need to be deal breakers. Tell customers immediately when an item is unavailable; search results screens and product details pages must clearly indicate that an item is unavailable. Customers should still be able to order temporarily unavailable items. (Explain when it will be available and any other relevant information.) Notify customers by email when an out-of-stock item becomes available. If you can't give customers exactly what they want, try to offer a substitute that is an appropriate match.

Chapter Ten

THE CONTINGENCY DESIGN TEST

See how your site rates

Now that you've read the guidelines, how can you apply them to your site? This Contingency Design Test is a series of tasks that will help you evaluate your site. Use it to identify your site's weak spots. Then improve them by following the relevant guidelines.

The tasks are separated into the following categories:

- Forms
- URLs
- Help
- Login
- Search
- Unavailable and out-of-stock items

WHO SHOULD PERFORM THE TASKS?

Start off with a self-diagnosis. Test your own site, and see how it performs.

Eventually, you'll also want to test customers and folks less familiar with your site. (Because you live and breathe your site, it's nearly impossible to maintain an objective view.) Outsiders will give you a fresh perspective and reveal issues that might otherwise go unseen.

You may eventually want to also test your competitors' sites to see how they compare. You may pick up some good ideas from their techniques.

HOW DOES THIS DIFFER FROM OTHER SITE USABILITY TESTS?

Many usability tests ignore failure scenarios. When a person gets off track, the test ends. This test begins where others usually end. It focuses exclusively on scenarios where customers make a mistake, encounter errors, or otherwise need help.

SCORING YOUR TEST

Here is how you should assign scores to tasks:

2 points	Site handles the task properly based on the relevant contingency design guidelines (thumbs up).
1 point	Site does a decent job of handling the task but needs improvement.
0 points	Site does not handle the task adequately (thumbs down).
N/A	Task does not apply to your site. Just remember to leave out these items from the total number of tasks used when calculating your final percentage.

For example, let's score "Browse site with images turned off." You should check to see whether your site uses ALT tags effectively according to Guideline 14, page 81. Then, score your site accordingly:

2 points	If your site uses ALT tags in accordance with the guideline
1 point	If your site uses ALT tags only half the time
0 points	If your site never uses ALT tags

THE CONTINGENCY DESIGN TEST

The following sections describe the tasks that will help you evaluate your site.

Category: Forms (18 tasks)

____ **Leave a required field blank.**
Is the error immediately noticeable? Is it properly displayed?
(Guidelines 1, 2, pages 18, 22)

____ **Fix a form mistake without going back to the previous screen.**
Does the error screen let you correct the problem field without backtracking?
(Guideline 4, page 29)

____ **Determine which fields are required in a form.**
Is it clear which fields must be filled in and which can be left blank?
(Guideline 8, page 58)

____ **Enter different formats for an entry.**
Are all common ways of entering an entry accepted—for instance, (212) 555-1212 and 212-555-1234?
(Guideline 9, page 61)

____ **Use a pulldown menu to select from multiple entry options**
Are pulldowns used to ensure valid entries?
(Guideline 10, page 64)

____ **Look for sample entries at potentially confusing fields.**
Are examples of proper entries provided?
(Guideline 10, page 64)

____ **Find form limits.**
Are character or entry limits displayed?
(Guideline 11, page 68)

____ **Enter too many characters in a text box.**
Is the MAXLENGTH attribute used?
(Guideline 11, page 68)

____ **Submit too many or too few entries in a form.**
Is the limit explained clearly?
(Guideline 11, page 68)

____ **Select an option that is not actually available.**
Are unavailable form options eliminated?
(Guideline 12, page 74)

_____ **Submit an email address with an invalid format (omit @).**
Does the site catch an invalid entry?
(Guideline 13, page 77)

_____ **Enter a date with an invalid format.**
Does the site catch an invalid entry?
(Guideline 13, page 77)

_____ **Enter a state and zip code that don't match.**
Does the site catch an invalid entry?
(Guideline 13, page 77)

_____ **Double-click the Submit button on a form.**
Is the form submitted twice?
(Guideline 14, page 81)

_____ **Click the Reset/Clear button.**
Can Reset/Clear/Cancel be eliminated?
(Guideline 14, page 81)

_____ **Start a lengthy form and complete it later.**
Can a form be saved and finished later?
(Guideline 15, page 86)

_____ **During a multistep process, use the Back button.**
Can you go back without a breakdown?
(Guideline 26, page 142)

_____ **Check the navigation options during multistep processes.**
Are links unrelated to the process eliminated?
(Guideline 30, page 156)

Category: URLs (3)

_____ **Enter a URL that doesn't work at your site.**
Is the "Page Not Found" screen effective?
(Guideline 16, page 92)

_____ **Search or navigate from the "Page Not Found" screen.**
Can you search or click to home?
(Guideline 16, page 92)

_____ **Enter a URL that is slightly wrong.**
Are you redirected to the proper URL?
(Guideline 17, page 99)

Category: Help (4)

____ **Answer a common question via the Help section.**
Is it easy to find answers?
(Guideline 21, page 118)

____ **Get help from a message board or online tutorial.**
Are self-help options offered?
(Guideline 22, page 123)

____ **Get help via nonsite options.**
Are other help outlets (phone, chat, and so forth) offered?
(Guideline 23, page 126)

____ **Send email to customer support asking for help.**
Is the response timely and effective?
(Guideline 24, page 130)

Category: Login (3)

____ **Log in using an invalid username or password.**
Is assistance offered for bad logins?
(Guideline 25, page 135)

____ **Obtain a forgotten username or password.**
Is there a way to retrieve lost/forgotten IDs and passwords?
(Guideline 25, page 135)

____ **Sign up with a username that is already taken.**
Are alternative names that are available offered?
(Guideline 40, page 212)

Category: Search (7)

____ **Find explanation when inexact matches are shown.**
Is a clear justification for the results offered?
(Guideline 31, page 162)

____ **Search for a term with zero matches.**
Is a clear explanation for the lack of results offered?
(Guideline 31, page 162)

_____ **Mistype search terms (typo, hyphenation, and so on).**
Are common errors mapped to right results?
(Guideline 32, page 168)

_____ **Filter a lot of search results down to a manageable number.**
Can you refine and filter results?
(Guideline 33, page 176)

_____ **Expand search results that are too limited.**
Can you easily expand search criteria?
(Guideline 34, page 187)

_____ **Find tips on how to improve searches.**
Is information offered for improving results?
(Guideline 35, page 190)

_____ **Find advanced search.**
Is the default search a simple one?
(Guideline 36, page 193)

Category: Unavailable and Out-of-Stock Items (5)

_____ **Try to find an unavailable or out-of-stock item.**
Is it immediately clear that item is unavailable?
(Guideline 37, page 200)

_____ **Get information about an unavailable item.**
Are item details still offered?
(Guideline 38, page 204)

_____ **Pre-order an item that will be available later.**
Are advance orders possible?
(Guideline 38, page 204)

_____ **Sign up to be notified when an item is back in stock.**
Is email notification offered?
(Guideline 39, page 208)

_____ **Find similar items that are available now.**
Are links to close matches offered?
(Guideline 40, page 212)

TALLY YOUR SCORE

To calculate your final percentage, do the following:

1. Add up your final score.
2. Divide your final score in Step 1 by the number of applicable tasks times 2.
3. Multiply that number by 100 to get your percentage.

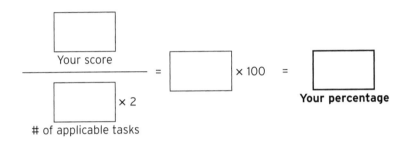

Here's an example: If 28 of the 40 action items applied to your site, and you scored 32 on those 28 applicable items, your contingency design score would be 57 percent.

SEE HOW YOU STACK UP

After you determine your contingency design score, use the following scale to see how you rate:

80% or higher	You're treating customers well, but there's always room to improve.
40% to 80%	Time to get serious—it's likely you're frustrating, and possibly losing, a lot of customers.
Below 40%	Get expert help and improve your contingency design before it's too late.

Conclusion

CONTINGENCY DESIGN
A Long-Term Commitment

So now you know the contingency design guidelines your site should follow. Just stick to the guidelines, use the contingency design test in Chapter 10, and you'll be all set, right? Well, not quite.

Sites evolve and change. You can't expect to ever be "done" with contingency design. Each time you plug a leak, a new one will spring up. It's the nature of the beast.

That's why you need to make error recovery and prevention part of your long-term design process. Here's how:

- **Study customer support inquiries.**
  Identify weak spots.
- **Solicit feedback.**
  Reach out to customers.
- **Analyze server logs.**
  Track the real usage of your site.
- **Look outside for help.**
  Get external input.

- **Put someone in charge.**
  The buck stops here.

- **Build a contingency design knowledgebase.**
  Track issues and solutions.

- **Prepare to fail.**
  Admit things will go wrong.

STUDY CUSTOMER SUPPORT INQUIRIES

Examine your site's email and phone inquiries and look for red flags. Which questions are asked most often? Which issues upset customers the most? Use this information to guide you as you improve your site's contingency design.

Pay special attention to any issues that produce a sizeable number of support questions. If customers keep asking about return policy details, for example, add this information to the FAQ section and/or checkout process. If a specific field on a form confuses visitors, provide contextual help near the field to make the form easier to complete.

SOLICIT FEEDBACK

Don't just sit around and wait for visitors to get in touch. Solicit feedback at error messages, Help sections, and other potential problem spots. Smart customers are like free usability consultants; they'll often reveal problems that would otherwise go unnoticed.

Where should you solicit feedback?

- Error screens
- Product pages
- Search results
- Help areas
- Support emails
- Any potential crisis points

Error screens

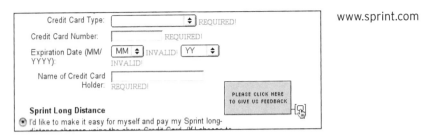

www.sprint.com

Error screens often confuse visitors. That's why Sprint offers a feedback link that "follows" visitors (via DHTML) around this error page. Customers don't have to stray to report problems or ask questions.

Product pages

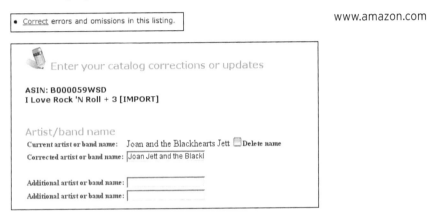

www.amazon.com

Any site that contains hundreds of items will inevitably display an inaccurate listing. Why not ask customers to help out when they spot such errors?

At the bottom of each Amazon product page is a link to "Correct errors and omissions in this listing." In this case, I clicked it because I spotted a mistake at a CD listing. ("Joan and the Blackhearts Jett" should be "Joan Jett and the Blackhearts.") The link takes me to a form where I can quickly notify Amazon of the slip-up. Make sure a staffer verifies the accuracy of any changes before updating the site, however. You'll open up a can of worms if you let visitors edit data directly.

Search results

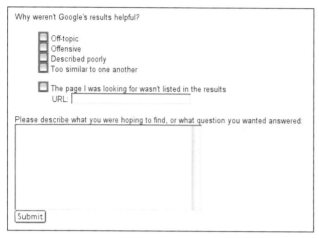

www.google.com

Dissatisfied with your results at Google? Each set of search results comes with a link to report any frustration. Click "Help us improve" and you can quickly tell Google which results you were hoping to find and why you were disappointed.

Join the search party
Our editorial and technical groups are always looking for ways to make your searches easier. If you have ideas to help us serve you better in this regard, please send feedback to the ZDNet Search Guru. Let us know how our search tool is working for you.

www.zdnet.com

ZDNet asks visitors for ideas on improving the search process.

Help areas

www.yahoo.com

Smart sites continually strive to find out whether their help is actually helpful. In this example, Yahoo! gives visitors a way to speak out about online help information. Customers can click on Yes if this help screen worked or No to explain shortcomings.

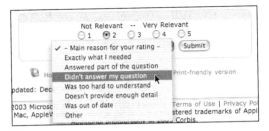

www.microsoft.com

Microsoft asks customers to rate the relevance of each help screen on a scale of 1 to 5. The use of radio buttons and a pull-down menu means customers can leave feedback quickly with just a few clicks. Microsoft also could offer a text box or feedback link that enables visitors to leave a more detailed comment.

Email support

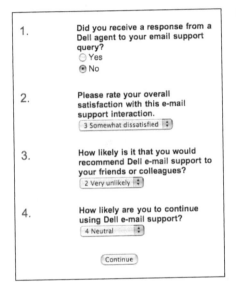

www.dell.com

Dell followed up on a customer support inquiry with this survey that asks me to rate the interaction. This is a nifty way to judge the effectiveness of your customer support communication.

Potential crisis points

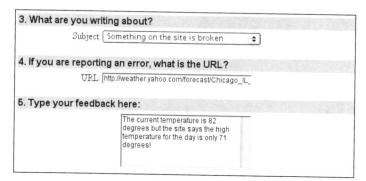

www.yahoo.com

The Yahoo! weather screen showed an obvious glitch. (The current temperature was higher than the high temperature for the day.) Just a click away from the weather page is a link to report the error. Feedback should never reside too far away from any potential crisis point.

ANALYZE SERVER LOG FILES

Server logs can reveal valuable contingency design clues. For instance:

- Which pages cause customers to bail out or seek help?
- Is there a search term that customers keep entering that isn't matching up with results?
- Is a conversion rate (for instance, the number of visitors compared to the number of purchasing customers) failing to meet expectations?
- Which FAQ topic gets the most visitor attention?
- Do visitors constantly click the definition for a specific term?

The answers to these questions will guide you to areas of your site that require closer examination.

The great thing about server logs is that they reflect *real* usage of your site. Unlike normal usability testing, logs show a large number of real visitors using your site in a natural setting over an extended period of time. You can't re-create that in a lab.

Standard site logs can contain extreme amounts of data, however. Larger sites may want to invest in a software package that will help capture the most relevant data.

GET OUTSIDE OPINIONS

How are other people doing it? When you need fresh ideas, experts and even competitors can help.

Expert reviews

Outside experts offer an objective, experienced viewpoint that you won't get from your in-house team. A good review will not only point out what's wrong but also include recommendations for how to improve.

What are the benefits of hiring an outside consultant?

- They have experience dealing with a wide range of sites.
- They can bring an impartial, detached viewpoint that is difficult to maintain when looking at your own site.
- They are immune to the internal political conflicts that can often cripple a project—they can be honest without having to worry about future repercussions.

Competitive analysis

Sometimes other sites can provide inspiration on sticky situations. Although you shouldn't plagiarize anyone's work, you can gain insight by watching how competitors and other successful sites handle crisis points. Problems with your checkout process? See how Amazon handles similar issues. Search confusion? Take a look at Google's techniques.

PUT SOMEONE IN CHARGE OF CONTINGENCY DESIGN

Because contingency design encompasses so many different areas of a company (for instance, programming, copywriting, and design), it's a good idea to assign someone to oversee the various efforts. This person should make certain everyone is on the same page and knowledge is effectively transferred among departments. (For example, get customer support to deliver relevant information to the engineers who can implement changes.)

Although "Chief of Contingency Design" probably won't be a full-time position, it's important to make sure the buck stops somewhere. If no one takes a companywide view of contingency design, troubles may linger or go unseen.

BUILD A CONTINGENCY DESIGN KNOWLEDGEBASE

Create a knowledgebase of contingency design issues and solutions. A knowledgebase is an interactive tool that allows site staffers to search and browse contingency design-related issues and solutions at your site. This database should be regularly updated. You also may want to give each issue an ID number for easier tracking.

A knowledgebase gives staffers a reference point so they won't have to reinvent the wheel each time a contingency design issue pops up. "How do we handle login errors?" "Check issue 24 in the knowledgebase."

PREPARE TO FAIL

Many companies are so focused on success that they ignore the reality of failure. To avoid this trap, create a culture that acknowledges that things will go wrong. Then, dedicate yourself to helping customers rebound when these troubles do occur.

CONCLUSION: ONE STEP AT A TIME

Whew. At this point, you may be asking, "Where do I even begin?" The task of improving contingency design at a large site is enough to overwhelm even the most enthusiastic site builder.

Start off by focusing on short-term wins. One of the best parts of contingency design is that even quick fixes can yield significant returns. Changing just one screen can dramatically reduce customer frustration. These early victories will build momentum and make long-term changes easier to pull off.

When it comes to contingency design, it's wise to remember the words of Chinese philosopher Lao-Tzu: "The longest journey begins with a single step." Tackle error messages, "Page Not Found" screens, and other low-degree-of-difficulty tweaks. You'll see a difference. Then take on bigger projects such as overhauling your Help section or humanizing your search engine.

Good luck!

INDEX

Peachpit
Essential books for the creative community

Visit Peachpit on the Web at www.peachpit.com

- Read the latest articles and download timesaving tipsheets from best-selling authors such as Scott Kelby, Robin Williams, Lynda Weinman, Ted Landau, and more!

- Join the Peachpit Club and save 25% off all your online purchases at peachpit.com every time you shop—plus enjoy free UPS ground shipping within the United States.

- Search through our entire collection of new and upcoming titles by author, ISBN, title, or topic. There's no easier way to find just the book you need.

- Sign up for newsletters offering special Peachpit savings and new book announcements so you're always the first to know about our newest books and killer deals.

- Did you know that Peachpit also publishes books by Apple, New Riders, Adobe Press, Macromedia Press, and palmOne Press? Swing by the Peachpit family section of the site and learn about all our partners and series.

- Got a great idea for a book? Check out our About section to find out how to submit a proposal. You could write our next best-seller!

You'll find all this and more at www.peachpit.com. Stop by and take a look today!

About

37signals

Matthew Linderman

Jason Fried

Chicago-based **37signals** (www.37signals.com) is a team of web design and usability specialists dedicated to simple, and usable, customer-focused design. 37signals popularized the concept of contingency/defensive design in various articles and white papers and via the web site DesignNotFound.com. The team also has conducted workshops and presentations on the topic for a variety of conferences and companies.

37signals clients include Microsoft, Qwest, Monster.com, Clear Channel, Panera Bread, Meetup, Performance Bike, and Transportation.com. Work has been featured in the *New York Times*, *Sports Illustrated*, *Washington Post*, on *CNN*, and in numerous other publications. Team members have appeared as featured speakers at AIGA Risk/Reward, Activ8, South By Southwest, HOW Design Conference, ForUse, and other conferences. Additional information can be found at www.37signals.com.

This book is authored by **Matthew Linderman** with **Jason Fried**. Other members of the 37signals team include Ryan Singer and Scott Upton.